日本語上級練習

STRIVE FOR A 5

AP* JAPANESE PRACTICE TESTS

By the Authors of the Bestselling Series *Adventures in Japanese*!

FIELD TEST EDITION

HIROMI PETERSON, NAOMI HIRANO-OMIZO & JUNKO ADY

Illustrated by Michael Muronaka

Cheng & Tsui Company
Boston

*AP is a registered trademark of the College Board, which was not involved in the production of, and does not endorse, this product.

Copyright © 2009 by Hiromi Peterson

All rights reserved. No part of this publication may be reproduced or transmitted in any form or by any means, electronic or mechanical, including photocopying, recording, scanning, or any information storage or retrieval system, without written permission from the publisher.

16 15 14 13 12 11 10 09 08   1 2 3 4 5 6 7 8 9 10

Field Test Edition 2009

Published by
Cheng & Tsui Company, Inc.
25 West Street
Boston, MA 02111-1213 USA
Fax (617) 426-3669
www.cheng-tsui.com
"Bringing Asia to the World"™

ISBN 978-0-88727-649-1

Illustrations by Michael Muronaka

All logos and references mentioned in this textbook are used for identification purposes only and are the property of their respective owners.

Printed in the United States of America

STRIVE FOR A 5: AP* JAPANESE PRACTICE TESTS
CONTENTS

To the Student and the Teacher

Acknowledgment

	Listening	聞く	1
	Reading	読む	28
	Writing : Text Chat	書く：テキストチャット	61
	Writing : Compare & Contrast	書く：比較と対比	75
	Writing : Cultural Topic Posting	書く：文化	91
	Speaking : Conversation	話す：会話	105
	Speaking : Return Telephone Call	話す：留守番電話	120
	Speaking : School Announcement	話す：お知らせ	135
	Speaking : Story Naration	話す：四コマ漫画	150
	Speaking : Cultural Presentation	話す：文化	165

Answer Key   180

Reference

DOWNLOADS

Users of this book have access to free, downloadable audio recordings that correspond to the listening sections. To download the audio files, you simply need to register your product key on our website.

Your Product Key: **UREM-U6ED**

Instructions for Downloading Audio Recordings:
1. Visit the Cheng & Tsui Download Center at http://www.cheng-tsui.com/downloads and follow the instructions for creating a Cheng-Tsui.com user account.
2. Register your product key.
3. Download the audio files.
4. For technical support, please contact support@cheng-tsui.com or call 1-800-554-1963.

TO THE STUDENT AND THE TEACHER

With the introduction of the AP* Japanese Language and Culture Exam in May 2007, students and teachers of Japanese were faced with the daunting task of preparing for this challenging opportunity. Teachers began networking in an effort to search for appropriate materials to prepare their students. In response to this need, we began writing two volumes, *Further Adventures in Japanese: Suitable for Advanced Placement Programs* and *Strive for a 5: AP Japanese Practice Tests.* It took a full year to prepare the content and design the structure of these materials, and yet another year to create, develop and field test the materials in our own classrooms. Now, we are pleased to be able to share this field test edition with you. As it is still being refined, we plan to continue testing it in our classrooms this coming school year. We also hope to add more materials while revising the materials you find in this volume, and welcome your input and suggestions.

In the AP Japanese Language and Culture exam, 21 AP topics are listed as possible exam subjects. The topics are: 1. Self, Family and Friends, 2. School and Education, 3. Daily Life, 4. Food, 5. Clothing, 6. Shopping, 7. Travel, 8. Transportation, 9. Home and Community, 10. Cities, Towns and Villages, 11. Nature and the Environment, 12. Weather and Climate, 14. Communication and Media, 15. Technology, 16. Rites of Life, 17. Leisure, Hobbies and Sports, 18. Family, 19. Work and Career, 20. Body and Health, and 21. Japan and the World. Students are tested on their listening, speaking, reading and writing skills. Students are also required to demonstrate their understanding of Japanese culture and express their opinions about aspects of the culture. All exams are taken by computer. Students must type all of their written responses.

Further Adventures in Japanese: Suitable for Advanced Placement Programs focuses on the AP topics, vocabulary building, important grammar points, and general review strategies. In order to provide additional practice tests, we created *Strive for a 5*. We have included 12 or more different samples for each section of the AP exam: Listening, Reading, Writing (Text Chat), Writing (Compare and Contrast), Writing (Cultural Topic Posting), Speaking (Conversation), Speaking (Return Telephone Call), Speaking (School Announcement), Speaking (Story Narration), and Speaking (Cultural Presentation). We put all the samples for each section together, instead of full-length practice tests, so that teachers/students can pick and choose the topics they need more practice on.

In addition, we encourage you to use the AP *kanji* list provided in *Further AIJ* and the sample tests which appear at the end of each of the seven lessons of *Further AIJ*.

All audio files and AP *kanji* flash cards which accompany *Strive for a 5* may be found at the publisher's web site, http://www.cheng-tsui.com/downloads. Please download any of the materials you will need from this site.

Since the AP Japanese exams are administered entirely by computer, we highly recommend that all of the practice tests provided in our texts be conducted in a venue that best replicates the actual test situation. This may not be possible for technical or logistical reasons, but we trust that teachers will devise ways to closely approximate the actual testing situation even during practice sessions.

When assessing your or your students' test responses, please refer to the AP Scoring Guidelines provided on the College Board web site http://www.collegeboard.com/student/testing/ap/japanese/samp.html?japaneselag.

Based on our experiences with the sample tests we have used in our classrooms, we provide here some tips for each test section, which you may want to consider as you use this edition.

Listening: Multiple Choice Questions (60 points)
The audio file for this section may be downloaded from http://www.cheng-tsui.com/downloads. For this section of the exam, the students listen to a passage or dialogue, which is only read once or twice. They must then respond to multiple choice comprehension questions given in English. On the AP exam, the questions are not asked until after the listening portion is complete, so students should not look at the questions prior to listening to the passage. Students are advised to take notes as they listen. Since the response time students are allowed for each multiple choice question is 12 seconds, teachers are encouraged to follow the time limits as well during practice sessions. Once students have answered an item, they are not able to return and correct themselves even if they later realize they have made an error. It is therefore important that the student be sure of their answer before making a choice.

Reading: Multiple Choice Questions (60 points)
For this portion of the test, students will read a passage which may be a letter, article, or an excerpt of a reading or story, then answer multiple choice comprehension questions asked in English. It is essential that students be able to read and know the meanings of all 410 *kanji* on the AP *kanji* list. This list, along with *kanji* compounds which employ these *kanji*, appear in *Further AIJ*. We recommend that it be used as a *kanji* study guide. These *kanji* are also available in flash card format to be downloaded from http://www.cheng-tsui.com/downloads. Please feel free to use the flash cards in ways that best supplement your curriculum.

Writing (Typing): Text Chat (30 points)
For this section of the test, students must participate in an exchange of text chat messages. Prompts are given one at a time, and students have 90 seconds to type each response. To be successful, students must have the ability to type accurately and quickly in Japanese. Students should be strongly cautioned to select the correct *kanji* when they convert from *hiragana* to *kanji* as they are typing. Proofreading is essential. Please carefully heed the advice at the beginning of this section of the book.

Writing (Typing): Compare and Contrast (15 points)
In this segment of the test, students are given two topics to compare and contrast.

They have 20 minutes to plan and type out a short essay in Japanese. The required format is to begin with an introduction, followed by three similarities and/or differences between the given topics, and finally, a statement of the student's preference for one of the two topics and the reasons for that preference. For this portion of the text, it is suggested that the student begin by writing an outline in the required format, then type the article. We also recommend that students practice writing this portion by observing the 300 - 400 character length so they will be accustomed to writing articles of the required length. As in the text chat task, students should be very careful about typing the correct *kanji* and proofreading them for accuracy. Please carefully heed the advice at the beginning of this section of the book.

Writing (Typing): Cultural Topic Posting (15 points)
For this part of the test, the student is given one broad cultural topic and is asked to choose one aspect of this broad topic to discuss in writing. It should be designed as a response to a web posting on that particular sub-topic. Students again have 20 minutes to plan and type this response. The student must begin with an introduction, state the one aspect of the broader topic which will be discussed, then name three characteristics of this sub-topic, and finally, express an opinion and his/her feelings about this sub-topic. As in the compare/contrast section, the student has 20 minutes to complete this task. The students should first carefully plan the response. Writing an outline is recommended before beginning. As in all of the writing tasks, students should pay special attention to using the correct *kanji* and be trained to write a response of between 300 - 400 characters. It is important that students have a broad as well as deep understanding of Japanese culture. Please carefully heed the advice at the beginning of this section of the book.

Speaking: Conversation (15 points)
The audio files for this section may be downloaded from http://www.cheng-tsui.com/downloads. For this section, students participate in a simulated conversation. Students are first given a very brief description of the situation and must listen to prompts which are each said once. After each prompt, students have 20 seconds to respond. Students respond to four prompts. This conversation is not a simulated phone call. It is important that students first listen carefully and comprehend the prompts, then respond clearly and quickly. Students must also be aware of whom they are responding to and use the proper speech style (*-masu* or *-da* style). It is strongly advised that teachers adhere to the 20 seconds response time during practice sessions as well. Please carefully heed the advice at the beginning of this section of the book.

Speaking: Return Telephone Call (15 points)
The audio files for this section may also be downloaded from http://www.cheng-tsui.com/downloads. For this portion of the test, students must remember that they first listen to a simulated phone message, then call back to

respond to the message that has been left for them. Students should greet the person they are calling, acknowledge the message and indicate that they are returning the call. The student responds to four prompts, and has a space of twenty seconds to speak after each prompt. The student must use the appropriate speech style when speaking. Students should be as accustomed to speaking in the informal *-da* style as in the polite *-masu* style. It is most important, however, that the student comprehend the native speaker who speaks at natural speed. This section checks the student's conversational skills in daily life situations. Please carefully heed the advice at the beginning of this section of the book.

Speaking: School Announcement (10 points)
In this portion of the practice tests, students are required to make an announcement in Japanese to a group of Japanese visitors to their school. Students are provided with all of the necessary information in English and must prepare a one-minute announcement. Students may make quick notes to use, then have one minute to record the announcement. Students should be careful to follow the format given in the instructions. Students should be comfortable saying dates (months, days of the month, days of the week) and times quickly and accurately. Please carefully heed the advice at the beginning of this section of the book.

Speaking: Story Narration (10 points)
For this portion of the test, students are presented with a four-frame comic strip. They have four minutes to study the pictures and prepare a narration of the "story" they create based on the pictures. Students will then have two minutes to record their narration. The polite *-masu* style of speech must be used for the narration. Students are tested on how well they can describe what they see. Please carefully heed the advice at the beginning of this section of the book.

Speaking: Cultural Presentation (10 points)
For this portion of the test, students must imagine that they will be making an oral presentation about a cultural topic on Japan. They will be provided with a specific topic and will present their own view or perspective of the topic and must be able to discuss five appropriately selected aspects of that cultural topic. The oral presentation should be prefaced with an introduction and finished with a conclusion. Students have four minutes to prepare the presentation and two minutes to record it. It is recommended that students write an outline during the preparation time. Students should be well prepared with a solid understanding of a variety of cultural topics. Please carefully heed the advice at the beginning of this section of the book.

Answer Key
For the benefit of the user, all scripts and multiple choice questions in the audio file and answers to the multiple choice questions have been included at the end of this volume. Students and teachers may use these answers to compare and check their answers and to identify any areas in which additional review may be beneficial.

Finally, we close by requesting comments, suggestions and feedback from all users of this edition. This particular version is our first attempt at responding to a need for AP Japanese exam preparation. We hope that it will raise the proficiency of all students of Japanese as well as broaden the minds and hearts of its student users. Since it is still a field test version, we will be happy to hear from you through the publisher about your ideas on how this edition can be improved. Please contact us with any comments or suggestions at editor@cheng-tsui.com. Thank you for choosing to use *Strive for a 5!*

がんばりましょう！

ACKNOWLEDGMENTS

The authors of this volume of *Strive For A 5: AP* Japanese Practice Tests* thank the following individuals for their contributions to this book. Their support is much appreciated.

- Michael Muronaka for the cartoon and icon illustrations.
- Keiko Kurose for writing the reading material on "Cellular phones."
- Satomi Wise for creating the reading material on "Jobs."
- Rika Onchi for proofreading the reading material on "International exchange."
- Chuugogu Shinbun for sharing the article on "My *Hashi*."
- Sam Kamasu for sharing his web article "Web Interview Article."
- Michael Lim '07 for sharing the speech he wrote while he was a senior at Punahou School.
- Jeff Ady for recording and editing the audio files.
- Misa Uyehara, Hiroki Shuto, Reona Ono, Jeff Ady for their voice recordings.

Hiromi Peterson, Naomi Hirano-Omizo and Junko Ady

<聞く Listening アドバイス>

You can download the audio recordings for this section from http://www.cheng-tsui.com/downloads.

【Knowledge/skills】
• Interpretive communication
• Comprehension; inference

【Format】
• Multiple-choice questions
• Several listening selections, 30-35 questions, 60 points, 30 minutes total
• Selection will be read once or twice.
• Taking notes is allowed and the notes will not be graded.
• 12 seconds to answer each question
• Not allowed to move back and force among questions.

【Suggestions】
1. Takes notes while listening.
2. Since the response time students are allowed for each multiple-choice question is 12 seconds, follow the time limits during practice sessions.
3. On the AP exam, the questions are not asked until after the listening portion is complete, so you should not look at the questions prior to listening to the passage.
4. Once you have answered an item, you are not able to return and correct it. Be sure of your answer before making a choice.

<1・聞く>

Listening: Home Delivery

(Narrator)   Now you will listen once to a prerecorded message.

<1・聞く (質問)>

Listening: Home Delivery

(Narrator)　Now answer the questions for this selection.

1. How many pieces of luggage did Ken take to the *Takkyuubin* counter?
    (A) Ken took one suitcase.
    (B) Ken took one suitcase and another fragile box.
    (C) Ken took two suitcases.
    (D) Ken took one fragile box.

2. What directions did Ken hear from the clerk?
    (A) To complete the form in pencil.
    (B) To complete the form with a red ballpoint pen.
    (C) To complete only the section inside the bold lines.
    (D) To complete only the underlined parts of the form.

3. What did Ken have to write on the form?
    (A) Receiver's address and full name.
    (B) Receiver's address, full name and telephone number.
    (C) Sender's address, zip code, full name and telephone number.
    (D) Receiver's address, zip code, full name and telephone number.

4. What address is Ken sending his luggage to?
    (A) A location where the zip code is 603-8024.
    (B) The west district of Kyoto.
    (C) The south district of Kyoto.
    (D) The receiver is Ken himself, but Ken sent it to Mr. Kondo's address.

5. When does Ken want the luggage delivered?
    (A) Ken wants it delivered between 2:00 and 4:00 p.m. on 4/1.
    (B) Ken wants it delivered between 2:00 and 4:00 p.m. on 4/2.
    (C) Ken wants it delivered between 4:00 and 6:00 p.m. on 4/1.
    (D) Ken wants it delivered between 4:00 and 6:00 p.m. on 4/2.

＜２・聞く＞

Listening: Internationalization of Sports

(Narrator)   Now you will listen once to a conversation.

<2・聞く (質問)>

Listening: Internationalization of Sports

(Narrator)   Now answer the questions for this selection.

1. What were the results of the recent sumo tournament?
   - (A)   A sumo wrestler from Eastern Europe won the tournament with 13 wins and 2 losses.
   - (B)   A sumo wrestler from Mongolia won the tournament with 14 wins and 1 loss.
   - (C)   A sumo wrestler from Russia won the tournament with 13 wins and 2 losses.
   - (D)   A sumo wrestler from Hawaii won the tournament with 14 wins and 1 loss.

2. Where are the recent foreign sumo wrestlers NOT from?
   - (A)   Mongolia
   - (B)   Russia
   - (C)   Eastern Europe
   - (D)   Hawaii

3. What characteristic of foreign sumo wrestlers impressed the man?
   - (A)   Their blue eyes
   - (B)   Their blond hair
   - (C)   Their hairstyle
   - (D)   Their Japanese language proficiency

4. What opinion does the woman have about the internationalization of sports?
   - (A)   She supports the internationalization of sports.
   - (B)   Japanese baseball players should not play in the American major leagues.
   - (C)   Japanese soccer teams should not hire foreign managers.
   - (D)   All sumo wrestlers should be Japanese.

5. What opinion does the woman have about the future of sumo?
   - (A)   There will be no Japanese wrestlers in the future.
   - (B)   Foreign sumo wrestlers will be excluded.
   - (C)   Sumo will become an Olympic sport.
   - (D)   Not many young Japanese can endure the vigorous sumo practice.

＜３・聞く＞
Listening: Speech

(Narrator)　Now you will listen once to a speech.

<3・聞く(質問)>

Listening: Speech

(Narrator) Now answer the questions for this selection.

1. What is this person's background?
   - (A) He is Korean and is living in Japan.
   - (B) He is a Japanese citizen, but his parents are Korean.
   - (C) He is ethnically half Korean and half Japanese, and is living in Japan.
   - (D) He is half Korean and half Japanese, and is living in the U.S.

2. What value did he learn from the Japanese side of his family?
   - (A) respect
   - (B) humility
   - (C) perseverance
   - (D) honesty

3. What value did he learn from the Korean side of his family?
   - (A) patience
   - (B) honor
   - (C) trust
   - (D) frankness

4. In what kind of situation does he experience inner conflict?
   - (A) When he follows Japanese values.
   - (B) When he follows Korean values.
   - (C) When he follows his own heart.
   - (D) When he is torn about which set of values he should follow.

5. What is this person's message?
   - (A) We should not discriminate based on race.
   - (B) We should understand other cultures.
   - (C) We should communicate more with people from other countries.
   - (D) We should travel and see other countries.

＜４・聞く＞

Listening: My Town

(Narrator)   Now you will listen once to a presentation.

<4・聞く(質問)>

Listening: My Town

(Narrator)   Now answer the questions for this selection.

1. What kind of town does this person live in?
   (A)   His town is a historically famous place.
   (B)   His town is famous for its natural beauty.
   (C)   His town is famous for an old temple.
   (D)   His town is famous for its unique animals.

2. What kind of place is his town?
   (A)   A famous shrine was built by the water.
   (B)   There is a fireworks show every weekend.
   (C)   There is a famous festival in the fall.
   (D)   Many foreigners visit his town.

3. What is one good thing about living on this island?
   (A)   People can swim in the ocean.
   (B)   People are kind.
   (C)   People can see lots of stars at night all year long.
   (D)   Vegetables and fish are fresh.

4. What is a major problem on this person's island?
   (A)   The number of tourists who visit this island is decreasing.
   (B)   Young people who leave do not return to the island.
   (C)   The fish they can catch around the island is dangerous to eat.
   (D)   The Japanese inns and souvenir shops do not have enough customers.

5. What is this person planning to do in the future?
   (A)   He does not want to leave this island.
   (B)   He wants to return to this island after college.
   (C)   He wants to return to this island after retiring.
   (D)   He does not want to return to this island at all.

＜5・聞く＞

Listening: College Entrance

(Narrator)   Now you will listen once to a conversation.

<5・聞く(質問)>

Listening: College Entrance

(Narrator)   Now answer the questions for this selection.

1. What is a description of the first exam the woman took?
   (A) The first exam was held in February.
   (B) The results of her first exam were very poor.
   (C) After receiving the results of her first exam, she decided to apply to two national universities.
   (D) After receiving the results of her first exam, she decided to apply to Osaka University.

2. After scheduling a second exam at Osaka University in March, what happened?
   (A) She took the exam and passed it.
   (B) She took the exam, but failed it.
   (C) She didn't take the exam because of a high fever.
   (D) She didn't take the exam because of a traffic accident.

3. What college did this woman go to?
   (A) She was accepted by a national university.
   (B) She was accepted by a private university.
   (C) She decided to reapply to Osaka University the following year.
   (D) She decided to attend a college prep school the following year.

4. What correctly describes this man?
   (A) He was strong in math and physics.
   (B) He wanted to study biology in college.
   (C) He wanted to attend a college on the East Coast.
   (D) He applied to eight universities.

5. What were the results when this man applied to universities in America?
   (A) Recommendations, an essay and an interview were required by all the universities he applied to.
   (B) The results were announced at the beginning of April.
   (C) He was accepted by all the universities he applied to.
   (D) He decided to attend the college that offered the largest scholarship.

＜6・聞く＞

Listening: Cellular Phone Etiquette

(Woman)   Now you will listen twice to the instructions.

(Narrator)   Now listen again.

(Woman)   (Repeat.)

<6・聞く>

Listening: Cellular Phone Etiquette

(Narrator) Now answer the questions for this selection.

1. What cellular phone etiquette is expected in restaurants and hotel lobbies?
   (A) No cellular phone use is allowed in either restaurants or hotel lobbies.
   (B) Talking quietly on cellular phones is allowed in both restaurants and hotel lobbies.
   (C) Cellphone use is allowed only in restricted areas.
   (D) Cellular phone use is allowed in hotel lobbies, but not restaurants.

2. What cellular phone etiquette is expected on public transportation?
   (A) People may use cellular phones on the bus.
   (B) People may use cellular phones on electric trains.
   (C) People may use cellular phones on bullet trains.
   (D) People may use cellular phones in a specific restricted area on electric trains and bullet trains.

3. What will happen to a person who uses a cellular phone while riding a bike in Japan?
   (A) It is permissible to use a cellular phone while riding a bicycle.
   (B) The cellular phone will be confiscated by the police.
   (C) The police will ticket the cellular phone user.
   (D) It is illegal, so the person is expected to stop, get off the bike, and use the cellular phone.

4. In which of the following places is cellular phone use allowed?
   (A) Schools.
   (B) Museums and theaters.
   (C) Airplanes and hospitals.
   (D) Priority seats area on the train.

5. What is the Japanese rule about using a cellular phone while driving?
   (A) There is no penalty.
   (B) One receives a warning from a police officer.
   (C) A fine has to be paid.
   (D) Imprisonment for a couple of days.

<7・聞く>
Listening: Announcement

(Woman)　　Now you will listen twice to a prerecorded message.

(Narrator)　　Now listen again.

(Woman)　　(Repeat.)

<7・聞く>

Listening: Announcement

(Narrator) Now answer the questions for this selection.

1. Where is this announcement being made?
   (A) on a bus
   (B) on a train
   (C) in a restaurant
   (D) in a concert hall

2. What is this announcement asking its audience to do?
   (A) To turn off their cellular phones in the special designated seating area.
   (B) To turn off their cellular phones inside the building.
   (C) To turn off their cellular phones as soon as they get on the train.
   (D) To turn off their cellular phones near the doors.

<8・聞く>

Listening: School Debate

(Narrator)   Now you will listen once to a school debate.

<8・聞く(質問)>

Listening: School Debate

(Narrator) Now answer the questions for this selection.

1. Which animal does Taro support cloning?
   (A) cow
   (B) sheep
   (C) pig
   (D) chicken

2. What is the reason why Taro supports cloning of animals?
   (A) Cloned animals are cheap to produce.
   (B) Cloned animals are easy to produce.
   (C) Cloned animals can survive in any environment.
   (D) Cloned animals solve the problem of food shortage.

3. What does Hanako support cloning?
   (A) cows
   (B) pets
   (C) mice
   (D) She does not support cloning.

4. What is Hanako's stand on cloning?
   (A) Clone technology should only be used to support people's lives.
   (B) Clone technology should only be used to produce more food.
   (C) Clone technology should only be used to help sick people.
   (D) Clone technology should not be used.

5. What is Taro's stand of cloning?
   (A) Clone technology should only be used to support people's lives.
   (B) Clone technology should only be used to produce more food.
   (C) Clone technology should only be used to help sick people.
   (D) Clone technology should not be used.

<9・聞く>

Listening: Gifts

(Narrator)   Now you will listen once to a report.

< 9・聞く (質問) >

Listening: Gifts

(Narrator) Now answer the questions for this selection.

1. Which of these is NOT a Japanese gift giving custom?
   (A) Japanese people give seasonal gifts twice a year.
   (B) *Ochuugen* is a seasonal gift given in the spring.
   (C) *Oseibo* is a seasonal gift given in the winter.
   (D) Japanese give seasonal gifts to people who take care of them.

2. To whom do Japanese people NOT give seasonal gifts?
   (A) To their parents.
   (B) To their relatives.
   (C) To their friends.
   (D) To their bosses at their working place.

3. Which of the following is the most appreciated by Japanese housewives as gifts?
   (A) Gift certificates
   (B) Beer
   (C) Coffee
   (D) Laundry soap

4. What item do Japanese housewives give most often as seasonal gifts?
   (A) Canned fruits
   (B) Cooking oil
   (C) Gift certificates
   (D) Healthy drinks

5. Why do Japanese people buy seasonal gifts at department stores?
   (A) Department stores will send them directly to the recipients.
   (B) Department store gifts are nicely wrapped.
   (C) Department store gifts are very economical.
   (D) Department store gifts are of excellent quality.

<10・聞く>

Listening: American Food

(Narrator)   Now you will listen once to a talk.

<10・聞く(質問)>

Listening: American Food

(Narrator)   Now answer the questions for this selection.

1. What food did this person enjoy when she ate at a restaurant in America?
   (A) steak
   (B) potatoes
   (C) salad
   (D) bread

2. What surprised this person the most at the restaurant she went to in America?
   (A) An American man was eating a cake with ice cream.
   (B) An American family was eating lots of food.
   (C) American children were eating a big cake.
   (D) Everyone was eating a big meal.

3. What food was strange to this person when she ate at a restaurant in America?
   (A) sweet beans
   (B) unsweetened beans
   (C) cake with ice cream
   (D) baked potato

4. When this person returned to Japan, what food did she want to eat the most?
   (A) sushi
   (B) white rice
   (C) noodle soup
   (D) miso soup

5. What kind of opinion does this person have about dining at American restaurants?
   (A) The workers at American restaurants are kind.
   (B) American restaurants should offer chopsticks.
   (C) Leaving a tip at the restaurant is reasonable.
   (D) Eating with a knife and fork is harder than eating with chopsticks.

<11・聞く>

Listening: Department Store Telephone Message

(Narrator)   Now you will listen twice to a prerecorded message.

<11・聞く (質問)>

Listening: Department Store Telephone Message

(Narrator)　Now answer the questions for this selection.

1. When is this department store closed?
   (A) Sundays
   (B) Mondays
   (C) Tuesdays
   (D) Thursdays

2. What are the business hours at this department store?
   (A) 7:30 a.m. to 7:00 p.m.
   (B) 8:30 a.m. to 8:00 p.m.
   (C) 9:00 a.m. to 7:00 p.m.
   (D) 9:30 a.m. to 8:00 p.m.

3. What special sale does this department store now have?
   (A) A back to school sale
   (B) A New Year sale
   (C) An end of the year sale
   (D) A spring fashion sale

4. What is on sale at the food corner?
   (A) Seafood bento sale
   (B) Hokkaido bento sale
   (C) Bento from various regions
   (D) Bento from various regions celebrating cherry blossom viewing

5. Which of the following information is correct about this department store?
   (A) The special event corner is located on the 7th floor.
   (B) The special event corner will end on Monday, April 10th.
   (C) The food corner is located on the second floor of the basement.
   (D) The food corner closes at 6:00 p.m.

<12・聞く>

Listening: Four Seasons

(Narrator)   Now you will listen twice to an announcement.

<12・聞く (質問)>

Listening: Four Seasons

(Narrator)   Now answer the questions for this selection.

1. Which is INCORRECT description of Japan?
   (A) Japan is a horizontally long island.
   (B) The climate of Japan differs considerably by season.
   (C) The climate of Japan differs considerably by location.
   (D) The four seasons of Japan are all beautiful in their own ways.

2. Which is an INCORRECT description of cherry blossoms in Japan?
   (A) Cherry blossoms bloom in early April.
   (B) Cherry blossoms start to bloom from southern Japan to northern Japan.
   (C) In Kyoto, Cherry blossoms bloom around the end of April.
   (D) The cherry blossom season differs from year to year.

3. Which is an INCORRECT description of the rainy season in Japan?
   (A) The rainy season starts around June.
   (B) The rainy season ends around the middle of July.
   (C) During the rainy season, it rains very hard all day long.
   (D) During the rainy season, it rains lightly all day long.

4. Which is an INCORRECT description of summer and autumn in Japan?
   (A) Summer in Japan is very hot and humid.
   (B) Typhoons come to Japan mostly during the summer.
   (C) Autumn in Japan is comfortable.
   (D) The autumn colors are beautiful.

5. Which is an INCORRECT description of winter in Japan?
   (A) The Snow Festival is held in Sapporo.
   (B) The Snow Festival is held in the beginning of February.
   (C) The statues at the festival are made of snow and ice.
   (D) There are more than a thousand statues at the Snow Festival.

<13・聞く>

Listening: Elections

(Narrator)   Now you will listen once to a conversation.

<13・聞く>

Listening: Elections

(Narrator)   Now answer the questions for this selection.

1. What is Ken's experience with elections?
   (A)   Ken never ran in an elction.
   (B)   Ken was successful at his first run for office.
   (C)   Ken was successful at his second run for office.
   (D)   Ken was successful in every election.

2. What is Mari's experience with elections?
   (A)   Mari never ran for office.
   (B)   Mari never voted in elections.
   (C)   Mari once ran for office, but she was not elected.
   (D)   Mari was once elected as a student body officer.

3. What is Ken's opinion about Japanese politics?
   (A)   More women should become interested in politics.
   (B)   Japanese politics are changing a lot.
   (C)   Japanese voters should decide on their prime minister by direct election.
   (D)   Japan should cooperate more with the rest of Asia.

4. What opinion does Ken express in this selection?
   (A)   Ken wants to become a politician.
   (B)   Ken thinks politics influences decisions on environmental issues.
   (C)   Ken supports the Republican party.
   (D)   Ken thinks that Mr. Gore should become president.

5. What opinion does Mari have?
   (A)   Mari thinks that more women should run for political office.
   (B)   Mari favors politicians who support poor people.
   (C)   Mari supports persons who thinks globally.
   (D)   Mari thinks that she should run for political office.

聞

<読む Reading アドバイス>

【Knowledge/skills】
- Interpretive communication
- Comprehension; inference

【Format】
- Multiple-choice questions
- Several reading selections, 35-40 questions, 60 points, 60 minutes total
- May move back and forth among all the questions.

【Suggestion】
You should be able to read and know the meanings of all 410 *kanji* on the AP *kanji* list. (This list, along with *kanji* compounds which employ these *kanji*, appear in *Further AIJ*. These *kanji* are also available in flash card format to be downloaded from http://www.cheng-tsui.com/downloads.)

<1・読む>

Reading: Web Interview Article

ハワイで活躍の日本人・ピーターソンひろみさん

Q：ハワイに来られて何年になりますでしょうか。
A：３６年になります。
Q：当初はどういう目的で来られたのでしょうか。
A：１９７０年ハワイ大学夏期セミナーに始めてハワイに来ました。大学カフェテリアで主人と出会い、翌年京都の大学を卒業。ハワイに７１年に来て結婚して、ハワイ大学教育学部外国語学科に入学しました。
Q：現在されているお仕事をご説明下さい。
A：プナホウ学園という私立校で日本語と美術としての書道を担当しています。
Q：ハワイで生活されて一番苦労されたことは？
A：やっぱり英語。今も苦労しています。
Q：ハワイで生活されて一番楽しかったことは？
A：好きな家族や友人がいて、好きな仕事が出来て、いろいろな人種のいい人達や生徒に出会える。運がいいとしか言いようがないです。
Q：ハワイへ来られる方へ取って置きの楽しみ方をアドバイス下さい。
A：観光地ばかり行かないで、いろいろな所を足で歩いて下さい。いろいろな発見があるはずです。最近、動物園近くの土曜の朝市は楽しいです。
Q：ハワイのお好きな場所を教えて下さい。
A：趣味はシュノーケルで、カイマナビーチホテルの前のビーチが大好きです。いろいろな色をした熱帯魚や大きい魚や可愛い魚達にも出会えて、運動だけでなく楽しめます。時に亀にも出会います。
Q：ハワイでお好きなレストランとメニューは？
A：カイムキにある Waiwai Thai というタイ料理のレストラン、グリーンカレーが最高です。癖になる味です。

アロハウォーカー　http://www.alohawalker.com

<1・読む(質問)>

Reading: Web Interview Article

(Narrator) Now answer the questions for this selection.

1. What is Mrs. Peterson's educational background?
   (A) She graduated from a university in Hawaii and then a university in Kyoto.
   (B) She graduated from a university in Osaka.
   (C) She graduated from the University of Hawaii with a major in foreign language education.
   (D) She majored in art at a university in Kyoto.

2. What is an accurate description of Mrs. Peterson's life?
   (A) Before she could not understand English, but now she does not have any problems with English.
   (B) She is enjoying her family and friends, but has a little problem with her job.
   (C) She feels lucky to have a good life.
   (D) She is still nervous about meeting people of different ethnicities.

3. What does Mrs. Peterson recommend to visitors to Hawaii?
   (A) People should visit the famous tourist attractions.
   (B) People should take a city bus tour.
   (C) People should visit the shopping center.
   (D) People should walk around the city.

4. What kind of restaurants and dishes does Mrs. Peterson enjoy?
   (A) She likes sushi at Japanese restaurants.
   (B) She likes noodles at Japanese restaurants.
   (C) She likes the green curry dishes at Thai restaurants.
   (D) She likes the green papaya salads at Thai restaurants.

5. What does Mrs. Peterson enjoy?
   (A) She enjoys fishing.
   (B) She enjoys snorkeling.
   (C) She enjoys swimming in pools.
   (D) She enjoys surfing.

<2・読む>

Reading: Magazine Article

好きなことなら努力出来る

第十五回　山村由美（２８歳）
現代美術展特別賞受賞者

みじめな子供時代

私はとてもおとなしくて内気な子でした。３つ上の姉がいて、その姉が何をしてもよく出来たんです。成績も優秀で、音楽や運動の才能もあって、両親は姉ばかり可愛がっていましたね。私は子供ながら姉に嫉妬をしていました。姉は美人で、性格も明るく、男の子にもよくもてていたし。私はいつも姉と比べられていたので、劣等感を持っていました。競争してもぜったい姉にはかなわないと分かっていたからです。でも、小学校５年生の時、校内絵画コンクールに出した私の絵が賞をもらったんですよ。あの時から両親も私を認めてくれて、それで自信も出て来ましたね。

絵で救われた青春時代

高校２年の時に、好きだった彼にふられちゃって、もう世界の終わりだと思いましたね。２年もつき合っていたし、まさか彼が私の親友を好きになるなんて、思いもしなかったですねえ。その上、同じ頃に両親が離婚をしてしまって、私はもう落ち込んでしまいました。人がだれも信じられなくなって、ひとり絵を描いていました。絵に集中している時だけ、全ての苦しさを忘れることが出来ました。

新しい自分に挑戦

大学では人とか物などの油絵を中心に描いていたんですが、最近風景の水墨画を始めました。美しい日本の山々を旅して、スケッチして来ました。自然の風景を描いていると、自然と一体になって全てを忘れてしまいます。美しい雲の中に浮かぶ山々をスケッチしていると、自分が空を飛ぶ鳥にでもなったような気持ちになります。絵を描き終えた時の心のうちからの喜びは、生きていて良かったと思う瞬間です。

<2・読む(質問)>

Reading: Magazine Article

(Narrator)   Now answer the questions for this selection.

1. According to the article, why did Ms. Yamamura always feel inferior?
    (A) She could not compete with her sister's achievements.
    (B) Her sister was very mean to her.
    (C) She was bullied in school.
    (D) Her teacher treated her as an inferior.

2. How did she gain confidence?
    (A) She excelled in sports.
    (B) Her grades improved.
    (C) She became popular with boys.
    (D) Her talent in art was recognized.

3. Why did she break up with her boyfriend when she was in the 11th grade?
    (A) Her mother didn't like him.
    (B) He developed an interest in her best friend.
    (C) She met someone else and she liked her new boyfriend better.
    (D) She was more interested in painting than in her boyfriend.

4. What is her new challenge?
    (A) To draw human figures.
    (B) To draw flowers.
    (C) To paint natural scenery.
    (D) To draw animals and birds.

5. What benefits did she gain from painting?
    (A) She was recognized by her school friends.
    (B) She found true joy in painting.
    (C) She was able to make her family happy.
    (D) She could find a better job.

<3・読む>
Reading: Letter

エリンさん、

　元気ですか。お久しぶりです。マサチューセッツ工科大学の生活はどうですか。冬休みに学校に訪ねて来てくれたのに、いなくて失礼しました。

　さて、今日学校で生徒に「火の鳥」というアニメを見せました。そうです。あなたが大好きだったあの手塚治虫の「火の鳥」です。アニメを見ながらあなたのことを思い出していました。

　あなたが高校二年の時にリー君と町田さんと一緒に、日米協会主催のジャパンボウルの州大会で優勝し、ワシントンDCであった全国大会でも優勝し、賞として日本旅行の航空券と旅費をもらって、一緒に日本に行きましたね。広島の私の兄のうちに泊まった時に「火の鳥」という日本語版の本が十冊ぐらい畳の上に置いてあったのを見て驚いていましたね。あなたが英語版の一冊を読んで感動し涙を流したことがあると話していたら、兄がその本の一冊をくれましたよね。その日本語版、読んでみましたか。広島で買った電子辞書の引き方にも、もう慣れましたか。私があなたになぜ日本の漫画やアニメがおもしろいか聞いた時、あなたは日本の漫画やアニメはいいメッセージがあって、愛とか友情とか未来とか宇宙とかいろいろな事について考えさせられると言っていましたね。広島の平和公園ではNHK放送局の平和番組の係りの人に日本語でインタビューされた時、上手に日本語で答えていたので、感心しました。広島の後も、京都、奈良、東京へ行ったけど、あなたは御台場にあったロボット博物館が本当に気に入ったようでした。「私の夢はロボットを作ること」と言っていましたね。ロボットの研究を続けていますか。ロボット第一号が出来ましたか。秋葉原へゲームを探しに行った時、興奮して「秋葉原に住みたい！」と言ってたのも忘れられません。どこへ行っても抹茶のかき氷を食べていたのも懐かしいです。最近、その「火の鳥」のアニメのDVDが出版されていると知り、兄に送ってもらいました。あなたにもぜひ見せたいですねえ。

　ボストンはまだ寒いと思いますが、体に気をつけて。また夏休みに帰って来る時には、学校に遊びに来て下さい。では、お元気で。

２月７日　　　　　　　　　　　　　　　　　　　　　　　　　　　橋本道子

<3・読む (質問)>

Reading: Letter

(Narrator)   Now answer the questions for this selection.

1. What year of college is Erin in now?
    (A) Erin is a first semester freshman at MIT.
    (B) Erin is a second semester freshman at MIT.
    (C) Erin is a sophomore at MIT.
    (D) Erin is a junior at MIT.

2. What kind of trip to Japan did Erin experience?
    (A) Erin's trip was a prize she won at the Japan Bowl state tournament.
    (B) Erin went to Japan with a teammate and her teacher.
    (C) Erin visited Tokyo first.
    (D) Erin visited Hiroshima first.

3. What happened in Hiroshima?
    (A) Erin stayed at her teacher's brother's house.
    (B) Erin bought the book "Fire Bird" at the bookstore.
    (C) Erin read ten volumes of a book titled "Fire Bird."
    (D) Erin was interviewed by a NHK news caster in English at the Peace Park.

4. Which of the following does NOT describe Erin's interests?
    (A) Erin is interested in Japanese traditional culture.
    (B) Erin is curious about robots.
    (C) Erin loves to play Japanese computer games.
    (D) Erin likes green tea shaved ice.

5. Why did this teacher write a letter to Erin?
    (A) The robot reminded this teacher of Erin.
    (B) The "Fire Bird" anime reminded this teacher of Erin.
    (C) Erin visited this teacher at school, but her teacher was not in.
    (D) This teacher heard that Erin is returning home for summer.

<4・読む>

Reading: My Hashi

マイはし

店にサービス呼び掛け

福山

飲食店に自分のはしを持ち込む運動を福山市で広げている市民団体があります。使い捨ての割りばしの使用を減らし森林資源を守るため、「マイはし」を持ってきたお客さんに食事代の割引やコーヒーのサービスなどをするよう、店側に呼び掛けているのです。

その取り組みを進める「ごみ5R推進本舗」の落合真弓代表(55)に話を聞きました。昨年六月から市内の飲食店に直接出向きお願いをしています。OKしてもらうと、年に四回発行している団体のフリー情報誌「eco lo-jin+α(エコロジン・アルファ)」に店の地図やサービス内容を掲載します。これまで期間限定を含め、約四十店が参加しました。

落合さんは「マイはしを持って行くと、初めのころは不思議な顔をされていたけど、最近は歓迎されるようになった」と、みんながマイはしを持つように意識すると環境にも優しいし、ものを大切にする事につながると言いました。実際に、マイはしを使う人が増え地域の意識も変わっていると感じました。

(中一・大友葵)

マイはし運動の広がりを話す落合代表⊕とメンバー (撮影・中3晃越正礼)

中国新聞「ひろしま国」

http://www.chugoku-np.co.jp/hiroshima-koku/

<4・読む(質問)>

Reading: My Hashi

(Narrator) Now answer the questions for this selection.

1. Who started promoting the practice of carrying one's own chopsticks?
   (A) A group of students
   (B) A group of teachers
   (C) A group of parents
   (D) A group of citizens

2. What benefits do restaurant customers get by using their own chopsticks?
   (A) The customers can get free chopsticks.
   (B) The customers can get a free cup of coffee.
   (C) The customers can get a discount coupon for the next visit.
   (D) The customers can get a free package of tissues.

3. How do the participating restaurant owners benefit?
   (A) The restaurants receive publicity in the newspaper.
   (B) The restaurants receive publicity in the promotion group's magazine.
   (C) The restaurants will be recognized by the city.
   (D) The restaurants will be recognized on a radio program.

4. What is the public's reaction to this movement?
   (A) More people started to use their own chopsticks at the restaurants.
   (B) So far 40 people have used their own chopsticks at the restaurants.
   (C) Restaurant owners didn't support this movement.
   (D) People often forget to carry their own chopsticks.

5. Who wrote this article?
   (A) A professional newspaper reporter wrote this article.
   (B) A senior citizen wrote this article.
   (C) A junior high school student wrote this article.
   (D) A high school student wrote this article.

<5・読む>

Reading: International Exchange

　夕陽丘高校は大阪府の公立男女共学の進学校である。関西空港からも電車で一時間ぐらいで、天王寺というJRの駅からも近く、便利で静かな所にある。明治39年（1906年）に女学校として始まり、伝統と歴史のある学校である。戦後、男女共学になり、現在は普通科のほかに音楽科もある。白く美しい7階建ての校舎には、コンサートホールやプール等の施設が素晴らしい。韓国への修学旅行、ニュージーランドへの英語研修旅行、ウィーンへの音楽研修旅行などもあり、国際交流も盛んだ。

　1学期から2学期にかけて、僕達は夕陽丘高校の音楽科2年生40人と3度のテレビ会議をすることになった。テーマは「卒業式」だ。目標の一つは、日米のそれぞれの卒業式を紹介し合い、文化の違いを理解することである。もう一つは、僕達の日本語卒業式で歌う歌を作り上げることだ。僕達が日本語で作詞をし、夕陽丘が琴や三味線などの和楽器で作曲する。5グループの5曲から1曲を選び、その歌を僕達の卒業式で歌う。

　第一回目のテレビ会議では「卒業式」について紹介し合い、2回目では曲を話し合い、3回目では発表をする。夕陽丘は僕達の卒業式までに選ばれた一曲の演奏ビデオを完成する。僕達の卒業式では、夕陽丘の演奏をスクリーンに映し出し、演奏を聴きながら卒業生全員で歌う。

　この交流のためにインターネットの掲示板を使ったり、パソコンや携帯を使うことになっている。どんな曲が出来上がるのだろうか。初めての経験なので、皆ドキドキワクワクしている。

<　5・読む(質問)＞

Reading: International Exchange

(Narrator) Now answer the questions for this selection.

1. What kind of school is Yuuhigaoka High School?
    (A) It is a co-ed public high school.
    (B) It is a co-ed private high school.
    (C) It is a music high school.
    (D) It is a very traditional girls' school.

2. Which of the following correctly describes Yuuhigaoka High School?
    (A) It's near the Kansai Airport, so it is a little noisy.
    (B) It has wonderful facilities such as a concert hall and a pool, but they are in a tall building.
    (C) It has a school excursion to Korea and China.
    (D) It has an English study tour to England and a music study tour to Vienna.

3. Which of the following is true about the teleconferencing project with Yuuhigaoka High School?
    (A) It will happen two times a year with 40 Yuuhigaoka students.
    (B) One of the goals is for Yuuhigaoka to use traditional Japanese musical instruments.
    (C) One of the goals is to create a Japanese graduation song for our school.
    (D) Yuuhigaoka students compose the lyrics and we compose the music for a graduation song.

4. Which of the following is NOT true about the series of teleconferencing sessions?
    (A) For the first teleconference, we introduce ourselves.
    (B) For the second teleconference, we will discuss a musical piece.
    (C) For the third teleconference, we will have a presentation.
    (D) For our Japanese graduation, Yuuhigaoka students will play the song for us from Japan.

5. What kind of technology will NOT be used by the students for this project?
    (A) We will NOT use the internet.
    (B) We will NOT use Skype.
    (C) We will NOT use our laptops.
    (D) We will NOT use cellular phones.

<6・読む>
Reading: E-mails

Message #1
差出人： まり
送信日時： １０月１日
件名： 待ち合わせ場所

明日、京都美術館へ行くことになってるけど、どこで待ち合わせる？京都駅の改札口付近でいい？九時にね。

Message #2
差出人： 村山
送信日時： １０月１日
件名： サッカーの練習

今日のサッカーの練習は雨のため中止します。次の練習は後ほど知らせます。

Message #3
差出人： 一郎
送信日時： １０月１日
件名： ひでき

ひできのことを聞いた？ひでき、自転車から落ちてけがしたんだって。昨日も今日も学校を休んでいたし、明日も休むらしいよ。でも、病院に入院してるらしいから、お見舞いに行こうか。

Message #4
差出人： えりか
送信日時： １０月１日
件名： RE:ごめん

私も明日いっしょに京都美術館へ行こうと思ってたけど、ちょっと急用が出来て、行けなくなっちゃった。ごめん。

Message＃５
差出人：　　　　　中村
送信日時：　　　　１０月4日
件名：　　　　　　RE:明日の試験

風邪をひいたんだって。明日の経済の試験は、風邪が治って学校に帰って来た時に、受ければいいよ。薬を飲んで、よく休むといい。早く元気になってね。お大事に。

Message＃６
差出人：　　　　　ともこ
送信日時：　　　　１０月4日
件名：　　　　　　RE:忘れ物

水玉の青と白のかさでしょ。喫茶店に忘れてたよ。私が預かっているから、今度会う時に持って行くね。

< 6・読む(質問) >

Reading: E-mails

(Narrator)　Now answer the questions for this selection.

1. Which message is from someone who cannot go to the art museum?
   - (A)　Message # 1
   - (B)　Message # 2
   - (C)　Message # 4
   - (D)　Message # 6

2. In which of the classes below will there be an exam tomorrow?
   - (A)　history
   - (B)　math
   - (C)　literature
   - (D)　economics

3. Why was soccer practice canceled?
   - (A)　The weather was bad.
   - (B)　The coach was injured.
   - (C)　There is an important exam on the next day.
   - (D)　The coach caught a cold.

4. Who has the blue and white umbrella now?
   - (A)　Mari
   - (B)　The receiver of the e-mail
   - (C)　Erika
   - (D)　Tomoko

5. Which message conveys an encouraging message to the receiver?
   - (A)　Message # 3
   - (B)　Message # 4
   - (C)　Message # 5
   - (D)　Message # 6

<7・読む>
Reading: Cellular Phones

　私の名前は桂子。私は毎朝、携帯の目覚まし機能を使って起きる。好きな音楽を聴きながら起きられるので、私のお気に入りの機能だ。家を出てから大学に着くまで、携帯にダウンロードした音楽を聴きながら、歩いた。昨日の夜、寝る前にネットオークションで買い物をしたのに、今朝歩いている時に、まだ料金を払っていないことに気がついた。携帯でお金を払うことが出来るので、すぐに終わらせた。

　夕方、授業が終わって携帯電話を見ると、友達からたくさんメールが来ていた。たいていメールの料金は、送信しても受信しても一通毎にお金がかかるので、送受信数が多い場合は、一カ月の料金が高くなる。でも、私の場合は大丈夫。携帯電話の会社に定額コース（一カ月３９００円）で申し込んでいるからだ。私はよく絵文字入りのメールを送る。

　私は学校から家に帰る途中、長い間会っていなかった友達に偶然会った。私の携帯のカメラで記念に一枚写真を撮った。私はブログをしているので、今日撮った写真をアップしようと思っている。友達と別れた後、コンビニに寄って雑誌を買った。おさいふケータイで払った。おさいふケータイはとっても便利だ。

　帰宅して、明日友達と渋谷のハチ公の改札口で待ち合わせをしているので、自宅から渋谷駅までの電車の乗り方を携帯電話で調べた。これで大丈夫。それから、彼氏と長電話をした。疲れたので、ブログはやめた。そして、寝る前に目覚まし機能をセットして、携帯を枕の横に置いて寝た。今、携帯はなくてはならない必需品だ。

＜7・読む (質問)＞

Reading: Cellular Phones

(Narrator) Now answer the questions for this selection.

1. What is Keiko's favorite cellular phone mode?
    - (A) Her favorite is the alarm mode.
    - (B) Her favorite is the shopping mode.
    - (C) Her favorite is the camera mode.
    - (D) Her favorite is the train timetable mode.

2. When did Keiko shop on the internet?
    - (A) Keiko shopped on the net auction last night and made a payment last night.
    - (B) Keiko shopped on the net auction this morning and made a payment this morning.
    - (C) Keiko shopped on the net auction last night and made a payment this morning.
    - (D) Keiko shopped on the net auction last night and is going to pay later.

3. How does Keiko pay for the cellular phone?
    - (A) Keiko is charged for every message sent, but is not charged for received messages.
    - (B) Keiko is charged for every received message, but is not charged for sending messages.
    - (C) Keiko is charged for every message sent and received.
    - (D) Keiko is charged a fixed rate for both sending and receiving messages.

4. Where did Keiko meet her friend, and what did they do?
    - (A) Keiko met her friend on her way to the university and they walked to the university together.
    - (B) Keiko met her friend on her way to the university and they took a photo together.
    - (C) Keiko met her friend on her way home and they went to a convenience store together.
    - (D) Keiko met her friend on her way home and they took a photo together.

5. What did Keiko not do last evening before she went to bed?
    - (A) Keiko updated her blog.
    - (B) Keiko set her alarm.
    - (C) Keiko talked to her boyfriend.
    - (D) Keiko checked the train schedule to Shibuya.

<8・読む>

Reading: Article

ニートとフリーター

　ニート（NEET、Not in Employment, Education or Training）という言葉は、英国で生まれた。ニートは、仕事もせず、学校へも行かず、職業訓練も受けていない若者のことである。日本でのニートは、2003年で約64万人もいるという。日本のニートは若者の2％ぐらいというが、英国には地域によって15～25％もいる。英国のニート問題はより深刻だ。

　フリーターと呼ばれている若者もいる。仕事をアルバイトのように次々変えていく若者のことである。フリーターという言葉は日本人によって作られた和製英語である。フリーターの数は約200万人と言われる。日本のフリーターは若者の7％ぐらいという。フリーターは会社にとても便利だ。フリーターは安い給料で雇えるし、保険も払わなくていいし、それにいつでも辞めさせることが出来る。フリーターの数はだんだん増えていっているようだ。そして、これは現代日本の大きな問題の一つである。

<8・読む(質問)>

Reading: Article

(Narrator)   Now answer the questions for this selection.

1. Which of the following descriptions of NEET is NOT correct?
   (A)   The word NEET originated in Japan.
   (B)   NEETs do not work.
   (C)   NEETs do not attend school.
   (D)   NEETs do not take vocational training.

2. Which statement about NEETs is NOT correct?
   (A)   There were about 65,000 NEETs in Japan in 2003.
   (B)   About 2% of the young population can be categorized as NEET.
   (C)   In some areas of England, as many as 15～25% of the young population are NEETs.
   (D)   The NEET problem in England is more serious than in Japan.

3. What description of freeters is NOT correct?
   (A)   The freeters change their jobs often.
   (B)   The word "freeter" was made in Japan.
   (C)   There are about 200,000 freeters in Japan.
   (D)   About 7% of the young population in Japan are considered to be freeters.

4. What is NOT given as a reason for companies who favor hiring freeters?
   (A)   The company does not have to pay a large salary to freeters.
   (B)   The company does not have to cover insurance for freeters.
   (C)   The company can fire freeters any time.
   (D)   The company does not have to train freeters.

5. Which statement accurately describes the situation for NEETs and freeters?
   (A)   The number of NEETs and freeters is gradually increasing.
   (B)   The number of NEETs and freeters is rapidly increasing.
   (C)   The number of NEETs and freeters is gradually decreasing.
   (D)   The number of NEETs and freeters is rapidly decreasing.

<9・読む>
Reading: Jobs

大型スーパーワイズ　ワイキキ店

㊗ ㋐　店舗スタッフ　1 レジ　2 接客販売　3 品出し　4 一般事務　5 清掃

働き方はあなた次第!! ライフスタイルに合わせて働けます!

学生さん、フリーターさんもみ〜んな活躍中!!ドンドン応募してネ!!

- 資格：　22:00 以降は 18 才以上
- 時間：　(早番)　9:00〜18:00
  - (遅番) 18:00〜翌 1:00
  - (営業時間)10:00〜翌 1:00
  - *時間、曜日応相談
  - *4 は 9:00〜15:00
- 給与：　時給 800 円以上
  - *22:00 以降 1,000 円以上
  - *高校生は時給 750 円
- 待遇：　能力次第で毎月昇給可能、制服貸与、交通費 15,000 円迄支給、ミニボーナスあり、社員登用制度あり
- 応募：　まずはお気軽にお電話下さい。HP からも応募できます。
  - (携帯、PC からも OK!!)

やる気のある人大募集!!
未経験者も安心して働けます!!

30 名の大量採用!!

時給	800 円以上	*22:00 以降は 1,000 円以上
		*高校生は時給 750 円

◇マイカー、バイク通勤OK!!

◇1 日 4 時間から、週 3 日以上で応相談！

◇土、日のみ勤務の方も大歓迎!!

W　ワイズ
W　ワイキキ店
TEL808-123-4567
http://www.WWW.com

< 9 ・読む(質問) >

Reading: Jobs

(Narrator) Now answer the questions for this selection.

1. What is the minimum number of hours this supermarket requires their applicants to work?
   (A) 4 hours
   (B) 10 hours
   (C) 12 hours
   (D) Not specified

2. Which benefit is NOT included?
   (A) Mini bonus
   (B) Transportation stipend
   (C) Uniform
   (D) Boarding

3. What is the difference between working conditions for minors and adults?
   (A) Working time
   (B) Wages
   (C) Promotion
   (D) There is no difference

4. What type of person is this supermarket looking for?
   (A) Motivated
   (B) Well-disciplined
   (C) Intelligent
   (D) Healthy

5. What does the supermarket suggest to interested applicants?
   (A) Send a resume by mail
   (B) Walk-in
   (C) Telephone
   (D) All of the above

<10・読む>

Reading: Resume (2 pages)

履歴書　平成19年11月17日現在

ふりがな: けん
氏名: スミス 健
生年月日: 昭和60年8月7日生(満22歳) 男・女

ふりがな: イースト　パロ　アルト　カリフォルニア　米国
現住所 〒96823: 1602 East St. Palo Alto, CA, U.S.A.
電話: 1-808-945-5801

ふりがな: とうきょうと たいとうく にしちょう
連絡先 〒110-37: 東京都台東区西町3丁目8番地6号
電話: 03-3875-6275

年	月	学歴・職歴など（項目別にまとめて書く）
		学歴
平成10	6	ホノルル市立 リンカーン小学校 卒業
平成12	6	ホノルル市立 ニューリバー中学校 卒業
平成12	8	私立 スティーブン高校 入学
平成16	6	私立 スティーブン高校 卒業
平成16	8	スタンフォード大学 地球科学部 入学
平成20	6	スタンフォード大学 地球科学部 卒業予定
		職歴
平成18	7	大松組　研究科インターン
		以上

記入上の注意
①鉛筆以外の黒または青の筆記具で記入。②数字はアラビア数字で、文字はくずさず正確に書く。
③※印のところは、該当するものを○で囲む。

読

自己紹介書

平成 19 年 11 月 17 日現在

ふりがな	けん	現住所 〒96823	イースト パロアルト カリフォルニア州	☎ 1-808
氏名	スミス 健		1602 East St. Palo Alto, CA, U.S.A.	945-5801

年	月	免許・資格・専門教育
平成14	7	普通自動車運転免許 取得
平成15	3	文科省認定 漢字検定 4級合格
平成17	3	文科省認定 日本語能力試験 2級合格

その他特記すべき事項

現在、海水の活用について卒業論文執筆中

得意な学科	スポーツ
科学、日本語	バスケットボール（学生時代バスケ部所属）
趣味	**健康状態**
読書 料理	良好（体力には自信があります。）

志望の動機

インターンでの経験を生かして、環境問題を解決し、社会の役に立つ仕事をしたい。

本人希望記入欄（特に給料・職種・勤務時間・勤務地その他について希望があれば記入）

地球研究室
本社勤務希望

通勤時間	約	時間 40 分
扶養家族数（配偶者を除く）		0 人
配偶者 ※ 有・無	配偶者の扶養義務 ※ 有・無	

保護者（本人が未成年者の場合のみ記入）

ふりがな		☎
氏名	住所 〒	

採用者側の記入欄（志望者は記入しないこと）

読

<10・読む(質問)>

Reading: Resume (2 pages)

(Narrator) Now answer the questions for this selection.

1. Where did Ken attend elementary school?
   (A) Palo Alto
   (B) Honolulu
   (C) Tokyo
   (D) Kyoto

2. Based on Ken's resume, which statement is NOT correct?
   (A) Ken graduated from a public middle school.
   (B) Ken graduated from a private high school.
   (C) Ken graduated from Stanford University.
   (D) Ken had an internship during his college life.

3. What special qualification does Ken NOT have?
   (A) lifeguard license
   (B) 4th level of *kanji* proficiency
   (C) 2nd level of Japanese proficiency
   (D) driver's license

4. What is NOT a correct description of Ken?
   (A) Ken likes science and mathematics.
   (B) Ken's hobbies are reading and cooking.
   (C) Ken belonged to the basketball club.
   (D) Ken is very healthy.

5. What kind of job does Ken want to do?
   (A) Ken wants to work in engineering.
   (B) Ken wants to work for a publishing company.
   (C) Ken wants to work in international business.
   (D) Ken wants to work on environmental issues.

<11・読む>

Reading: Invitation Letter

拝啓　緑が眩しい季節になりました
皆様には増々ご清祥の事と御喜び申し上げます
さて　この度私たちは結婚することとなりました
つきましては　日ごろお世話になっている皆様に
結婚の証人としてご列席賜りたく　お願い申し上げます

挙式後は心ばかりの披露宴を催したいと思っております
お忙しいところ恐縮ですが
ご出席いただけましたら幸いです
　　　　　　　　　　　　　　　敬具
　　　　　平成20年5月吉日
　　　　　山本　一郎　　　　松田　春子

　　　　†††　日時　†††
　　　平成20年6月23日（日曜日）
　　　　人前結婚式　午前１１時
　　　　披露宴　　　午後１２時

　　　　†††　場所　†††
　　　　サンシャインホテル
　　　　オーキッドの間
　　　東京都新宿区高田馬場２丁目５番８号
　　　　Tel ０３-３２０７-０５４７

なお　誠に恐れ入りますが５月３０日までにご返事をいただければ
　　　　　　幸いに存じます

<11・読む(質問)>

Reading: Invitation Letter

(Narrator) Now answer the questions for this selection.

1. What event is this invitation for?
   (A) funeral
   (B) wedding
   (C) birthday party
   (D) anniversary

2. When is this event?
   (A) May 20th
   (B) May 23rd
   (C) June 23rd
   (D) May 30th

3. Where will this event be held?
   (A) Sunshine Hotel in Kyoto
   (B) Orchid Hotel in Shinjuku
   (C) Orchid Restaurant in Tokyo
   (D) Orchid Room of the Sunshine Hotel in Shinjuku

4. What is the setting for this event?
   (A) The ceremony will be held at a church.
   (B) The ceremony will be held in front of the participants.
   (C) The party will be held at the hotel garden.
   (D) The party will be held at a restaurant in the hotel.

5. What is this letter requesting?
   (A) Not to bring flowers.
   (B) To respond by May 30th.
   (C) Not to give money.
   (D) To attend the event in casual attire.

<12・読む>

Reading: Cherry Blossom

　「桜」というJ-Popの曲を最近の若者がよく作り歌う。歌のテーマはだいたい「別れ」と「門出」のようだ。桜が咲く季節はだいたい3月の下旬から4月の上旬で、日本の学校の卒業式と新学期に重なる。日本人が桜を見る時、桜の中で撮った友との卒業の記念写真や、桜の木の下でお母さんと一緒に撮った入学式の時の写真を、懐かしく思い出すはずだ。日本人にとって桜の花は特別だ。

　桜が満開になるころ、日本人は「お花見」を楽しむ。満開の桜の花の中で、家族や友人や会社の仲間達とお弁当を食べたり、お酒を飲んだり、カラオケをしたり、時を忘れて楽しむ。桜の花の下で、茶会を楽しむ人達もいる。ぜいたくなことだ。

　侍は、桜のようにぱっと咲いてぱっと散る人生を理想とした。一生懸命に生き、花を咲かせ、そして、いさぎよく死んで行く人生に美しさを見つけた。昔も現代も、桜の美しさ、はかなさを日本人は好む。桜の花が咲くためには、冬の寒さが必要だそうだ。人生も桜と同じに違いない。冬のような寒さがあってこそ、自分の花を咲かせられると思う。

<12・読む(質問)>

Reading: Cherry Blossom

(Narrator) Now answer the questions for this selection.

1. What kinds of themes are used in songs associated with cherry blossoms?
   - (A) Love and memories
   - (B) Separation and happiness
   - (C) Separation and new beginnings
   - (D) Youth and friendship

2. In what season do cherry blossoms bloom in Japan?
   - (A) Generally between the end of March and the middle of April
   - (B) Generally between the beginning of March and the end of April
   - (C) About the same time as the school graduation ceremony and the new school year.
   - (D) About the same time as Golden Week.

3. What activites do Japanese people enjoy outdoors while they view cherry blossoms?
   - (A) Singing *karaoke*
   - (B) Drinking sake
   - (C) Having a tea ceremony
   - (D) All of the above

4. What characteristic of cherry blossoms has attracted Japanese people?
   - (A) The elegance of cherry blossoms
   - (B) The short life span of cherry blossoms
   - (C) The beautiful color of cherry blossoms
   - (D) That they are a symbol of new life

5. What does the writer want to say in this article?
   - (A) People can achieve success by enduring hardships.
   - (B) People can be happy when they work together well.
   - (C) The cherry blossom season brings happiness to people.
   - (D) People who live a short life appreciate their lives most.

<13・読む>

Reading: Article

　最近、地球温暖化という言葉をよく聞く。自動車などから出る排気ガスが理由で、空気中に二酸化炭素が増え、大気が温かくなるという問題だ。

　地球の大気が温かくなると、どうなるのか。まず、北極や南極の氷河が溶け出すらしい。そして、海面が高くなり、低い土地が海に沈む。それに、高温による森林火災や、台風や竜巻きが多くなり、大雨による洪水が増え、干ばつで食べ物が少なくなるそうだ。こわい話だ。

　では、どうすればいいのか。この地球温暖化を解決するために、1997年に各国がどれだけのCO_2を減らすべきか京都議定書が作られたそうだ。2002年の統計によると、CO_2を一番多く出している国はアメリカ、二番目は中国、三番目はロシア、四番目は日本だそうだ。しかし、国によって、協力する国、しない国があるのは、驚くべきことだ。各国のそれぞれの理由があっても、地球を守るために、わがままな事を言っている時ではないと思う。

　私はこの地球温暖化の問題を知った後、自動車のガソリンをあまり使わないようにすることにした。そして、皆、低公害車を使うべきだ。そして、たくさんの物を使うことを豊かと思わないで、物を大事にすることを豊かと思える価値観を持つことが大切だと思う。

　　参考：マイロク先生の地球一よくわかる温暖化問題
　　　　　http://www.team-6.net/-6sensei/

<13・読む(質問)>

Reading: Article

(Narrator) Now answer the questions for this selection.

1. What is this article about?
   (A) The natural environment should be protected.
   (B) Recycling is important.
   (C) Energy is a big issue.
   (D) Global warming is a very serious problem.

2. What is NOT related to global warming?
   (A) Glaciers will melt and the sea level will rise.
   (B) We will have more forest fires.
   (C) We will have more earthquakes.
   (D) Food will become scarce.

3. What is true about the Kyoto Protocol?
   (A) According to the survey, Japan produced the third most CO_2 of all the countries in the world.
   (B) The Kyoto Protocol was established in order to solve global warming.
   (C) America supported the Kyoto Protocol.
   (D) The Kyoto Protocol was established in 2002.

4. What did the writer decide to do?
   (A) The writer decided to buy a hybrid car.
   (B) The writer decided to use less gasoline.
   (C) The writer decided to use public transportation.
   (D) The writer decided to walk more.

5. What did the writer suggest to the readers?
   (A) We should change our values and what it means to have a rich life.
   (B) We should use less energy.
   (C) We should educate people more about sustainability.
   (D) We should recycle more.

<14・読む>

Reading: Sweets

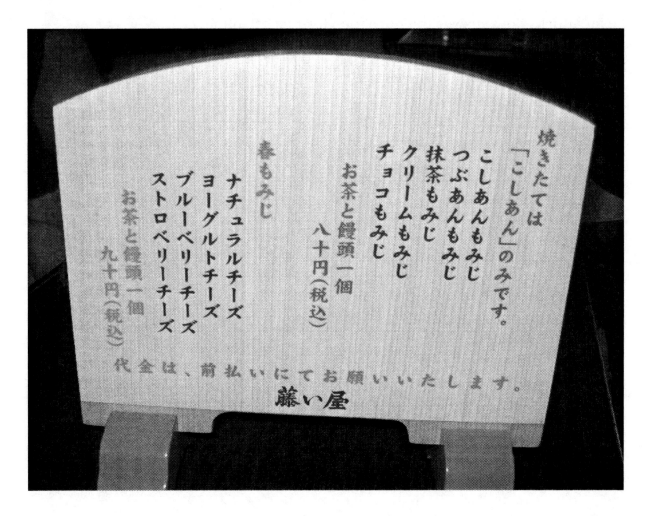

焼きたては「こしあん」のみです。

こしあんもみじ
つぶあんもみじ
抹茶もみじ
クリームもみじ
チョコもみじ

お茶と饅頭一個
八十円（税込）

春もみじ
ナチュラルチーズ
ヨーグルトチーズ
ブルーベリーチーズ
ストロベリーチーズ

お茶と饅頭一個
九十円（税込）

代金は、前払いにてお願いいたします。

藤い屋

<14・読む(質問)>

Reading: Sweets

(Narrator)   Now answer the questions for this selection.

1. What kind of sweets does this menu offer?
   (A) maple leaf shaped sweets
   (B) plum flower shaped sweets
   (C) fan shaped sweets
   (D) peach shaped sweets

2. Which flavor of sweets is NOT listed?
   (A) green tea
   (B) chocolate
   (C) coffee
   (D) red bean paste

3. What flavor of sweets do they NOT have in the spring?
   (A) strawberry cheese
   (B) lemon cheese
   (C) blueberry cheese
   (D) yogurt cheese

4. What can you order for 90 yen at this shop?
   (A) one regular sweet and a cup of tea including tax
   (B) one cheese flavored sweet and a cup of tea excluding tax
   (C) one regular sweet and a cup of tea excluding tax
   (D) one cheese flavored sweet and a cup of tea including tax

5. Which special note appears on this menu?
   (A) You must pay after eating.
   (B) You must pay before eating.
   (C) Only cheese flavored spring sweets are freshly baked.
   (D) Only regular sweets offered all year long are freshly baked.

<15・読む>

Reading: Travel Guide

世界遺産・歴史の道・熊野古道　ウォーキングプラン

古道ガイドと歩く悠久の旅

熊野古道の中でもアップダウンが比較的少ないと言われている約7kmのコース。古道の名所の説明などを聞きながら歩いていただいた後は昼食。そして西日本最大級の露天風呂に入浴できます。

※1名様よりお申し込みいただけます。

■設定期限：4月1日～9月30日の土・日曜日
■除外日：5月6日、8月12日・13日

旅行代金お一人（おとな・こども共）　6,500円

■旅行代金に含まれるもの
　☆3時間程度の熊野古道散策（古道ガイド付き）
　☆わたらせ温泉露天風呂での入浴と昼食
　　食事メニュー：おとな・こども共　田舎定食
　　（めはりずし、さんまずし、うどん）
　☆行程中のジャンボタクシー又はタクシー又はバス代

■行程

本宮大社	＝	発心門王子(ほっしんもんおうじ)	・・・	本宮大社	＝	渡瀬温泉（昼食・入浴）	＝	本宮大社
8:45 集合 9:00 出発		9:15		12:30頃	12:45頃	13:45頃		14:00頃

※古道を歩く時間はご参加いただくお客様により多少前後いたします。
※山道を歩きますので、歩きなれた靴でご参加ください。
※行程中のタクシーまたはジャンボタクシー又はバスは相乗りです。
※最小催行人員は6名です。
※小雨の場合は、催行します。
※古道ガイドはお客様の貸切ではございません。
※台風など荒天の場合は、中止の場合があります。

<15・読む(質問)>

Reading: Travel Guide

(Narrator) Now answer the questions for this selection.

1. What kind of tour does this travel guide introduce?
   (A) Visiting famous temples
   (B) A city tour
   (C) Climbing famous mountains
   (D) Walking historical mountain paths

2. When is this tour available?
   (A) Weekdays between April 1st and September 30th
   (B) Weekends between April 1st and September 30th
   (C) Weekends between April 1st and September 30th except on three days
   (D) All weekdays and May 6th, August 12th and 13th

3. What is included in the tour fee?
   (A) Taxi or bus fare
   (B) Snacks
   (C) Lunch
   (D) Bathing in a hot spring

4. Which of the following is NOT correct?
   (A) The meeting time is 9:00 a.m.
   (B) The departure time is 9:15 a.m.
   (C) Lunch time is around 1:45 p.m.
   (D) The return time is 3:00 p.m.

5. Which of the following is correct?
   (A) One should wear comfortable shoes.
   (B) The maximum number of people taken on this tour is six.
   (C) In case of light rain, the tour will be canceled.
   (D) The cost of the tour is different for adults and children.

<書く Text Chat アドバイス>

【Knowledge/skills】
- Interpersonal communication
- Informing; describing; explaining; expressing a preference; elaborating; justifying opinion; requesting; inviting; suggesting

【Format】
- 6 questions x 90 seconds, 30 points, 10 minutes total

【Speech style】
When you communicate with someone you don't know well, use the polite です/ます form. When you communicate with someone superior to you, use the honorific form, although it is not required by the AP exam. When you communicate with someone close to you, use the informal form, although it is not commonly required on the AP exam.

【Suggestion】
1. Each answer counts as five points, which means each response matters. Elaborate and answer throughly. Do not leave any section unanswered.
2. When you introduce yourself, it is polite and natural to say どうぞよろしくお願いします after giving your name.
3. At the closing of the entire conversation, show appreciation to the person with whom you are having a text chat. If you enjoyed the conversation, say 楽しかったです。 If you want to offer encouragement to your partner, say がんばって下さい。

＜１・書く（テキストチャット）＞　　30点　90秒x6

Text Chat : Introduction

You will participate in a simulated exchange of text-chat messages. Each time it is your turn to write, you will have 90 seconds. You should respond as fully and as appropriately as possible.

You will have a conversation about yourself with Maki Matsumoto, a student from your sister school in Japan.

1. Respond. (90 seconds)

    初めまして。山田です。どうぞよろしく。自己紹介、御願いします。

2. Describe. (90 seconds)

    そうですか。御家族について教えて下さい。

3. Give a specific example. (90 seconds)

    そうですか。子供の時、どんな子供だったんですか。

4. Explain your preference. (90 seconds)

    そうですか。今趣味と勉強とどちらの方が大切だと思いますか。

5. Justify your opinion. (90 seconds)

    今、どんな友達がいますか。本音を言える友達がいますか。

6. Ask a specific question. (90 seconds)

    最後になりますが、私について何か質問がありますか。

書：テキストチャット

＜２・書く（テキストチャット）＞
Text Chat: Japanese Study

30点
90秒 x 6

You will participate in a simulated exchange of text-chat messages. Each time it is your turn to write, you will have 90 seconds. You should respond as fully and as appropriately as possible.

You will have a conversation about your Japanese study with Aya Tanaka, a student in Japan.

1. Respond. (90 seconds)

   田中あやです。よろしく御願いします。日本語は何年ぐらい習っているんですか。

2. Give a specific example. (90 seconds)

   日本語の勉強は難しいですか。日本語は何が一番難しいですか。

3. Explain your reason. (90 seconds)

   なぜ日本語を取ることに決めたんですか。

4. Describe your teacher. (90 seconds)

   日本語の先生はどんな先生ですか。

5. Describe your experience. (90 seconds)

   日本語を習って、良かったと思ったことがありますか。どんな時か話を聞かせて下さい。

6. Explain your preference. (90 seconds)

   もし次の休みに日本へ行けたら、日本でどんな事をしてみたいですか。

書：テキストチャット

＜３・書く（テキストチャット）＞

Text Chat: Home and Community

30点
90秒 x 6

You will participate in a simulated exchange of text-chat-messages. Each time it is your turn to write, you will have 90 seconds. You should respond as fully and as appropriately as possible.

You will have a conversation about your house and community with Shota Nakamura, a student from Japan who will homestay at your house.

1. Respond. (90 seconds)

    初めまして。中村です。よろしくお願いします。来週から、お宅にお世話になります。いろいろ質問してもいいですか。

2. Describe a specific information. (90 seconds)

    まず、最初の質問です。どんな家に住んでいますか。ちょっと教えて下さい。

3. Give a specific response. (90 seconds)

    そうですか。ちょっと変な質問ですが、お宅ではくつをどこでぬぐんですか。

4. Give a specific response. (90 seconds)

    分かりました。家から学校まで遠いですか。通学にどのぐらいかかりますか。毎朝、何時ごろ家を出るんですか。

5. Give your opinion. (90 seconds)

    分かりました。もし、僕が一人で買物に出かけたかったら、歩いて行けますか。お宅は便利な所にありますか。

6. Ask a specific question. (90 seconds)

    もっとよく分かりました。有難うございます。僕について何か知りたいことがありますか。

書：テキストチャット

<4・書く（テキストチャット）>

Text Chat: Recycling

30点
90秒 x 6

You will participate in a simulated exchange of text-chat messages. Each time it is your turn to write, you will have 90 seconds. You should respond as fully and as appropriately as possible.

You will have a conversation about recycling with Daisuke Matsuda, a Japanese newspaper reporter.

1. Respond. (90 seconds)

    初めまして。日本新聞の松田です。どうぞよろしくお願いします。今日はそちらのリサイクルについて教えて下さい。

2. Give a specific example. (90 seconds)

    うちでどんなリサイクルをしていますか。

3. State your opinion. (90 seconds)

    うちでのリサイクルについて、あなたの意見を聞かせて下さい。

4. Give a specific example. (90 seconds)

    学校でもリサイクルとか環境のために何かしていますか。

5. State your opinion. (90 seconds)

    日本のリサイクルとアメリカのリサイクルを比べて、どう思いますか。

6. Respond. (90 seconds)

    最後になりますが、日本のリサイクルについて何か質問がありますか。

書：テキストチャット

<5・書く（テキストチャット）>

Text Chat: Clothing

30点
90秒 x 6

You will participate in a simulated exchange of text-chat messages. Each time it is your turn to write, you will have 90 seconds. You should respond as fully and as appropriately as possible.

You will have a conversation about clothing with Natsumi Iwasaki, a student in Japan who is going to study at your school.

1. Respond. (90 seconds)

    岩崎（いわさき）です。よろしくお願いします。そちらの学校に一学期留学することになりました。ちょっとどんな服を用意したらいいか教えて下さい。

2. Give a specific example. (90 seconds)

    学校には制服があるんですか。あれば、どんな制服ですか。

3. Give a specific example. (90 seconds)

    分かりました。今そちらで女子学生はどんな格好（かっこう）をしているんですか。何か流行（はや）っているファッションとかありますか。

4. Explain your preference. (90 seconds)

    ああ、そうですか。そちらは冬どのぐらい寒くなりますか。冬のファッションと夏のファッションとどちらの方が好きですか。

5. Justify your opinion. (90 seconds)

    分かりました。そちらで服を買いたかったら、町にどこかいいお店がありますか。

6. Ask a specific question. (90 seconds)

    ありがとうございました。日本のファッションについて何か質問がありますか。

書：テキストチャット

＜6・書く（テキストチャット）＞

Text Chat: Cellular Phones

30点
90秒 x 6

You will participate in a simulated exchange of text-chat messages. Each time it is your turn to write, you will have 90 seconds. You should respond as fully and as appropriately as possible.

You will have a conversation about cellular phones with Mari, a student in Japan.

1. Respond. (90 seconds)

   まりです。どうぞよろしく。最初の質問です。携帯電話を使い始めたのは、いくつぐらいの時でしたか。

2. Give a specific example. (90 seconds)

   そうですか。一番よく使う携帯の機能は何ですか。

3. Give a specific example. (90 seconds)

   そうですか。毎月携帯電話にどのぐらい払っているんですか。

4. State your opinion. (90 seconds)

   ああ、そうですか。携帯を使って、何か問題が起こっていませんか。

5. State your preference. (90 seconds)

   日本の携帯を見たことがありますか。日本の携帯とアメリカの携帯と何が違うでしょうね。

6. Ask a question. (90 seconds)

   最後になりますが、日本の携帯電話について何か質問がありますか。

書：テキストチャット

<7・書く（テキストチャット）>

Text Chat: Computers

30点
90秒 x 6

You will participate in a simulated exchange of text-chat messages. Each time it is your turn to write, you will have 90 seconds. You should respond as fully and as appropriately as possible.

You will have a conversation about your computer use with Yuta Watanabe, a student in Japan.

1. Respond. (90 seconds)

    渡部裕太（わたなべゆうた）です。どうぞよろしく。コンピューターの使用についてちょっと教えて下さい。

2. Give a specific response. (90 seconds)

    まず、毎日コンピューターをよく使っていますか。コンピューターを何のために使っているんですか。

3. Give a specific example. (90 seconds)

    ああ、そうですか。学校でコンピューターを使う時に、何か問題がありますか。

4. Give a specific example. (90 seconds)

    そうですか。コンピューターはいろいろ問題点も多いようですが、今、何が一番問題ですか。

5. State your opinion. (90 seconds)

    ところで、日本語のウェブページを見たりしますか。どう思いますか。

6. Ask a specific question. (90 seconds)

    いろいろ教えてくれてありがとう。最後に何か日本語のコンピューターについて質問がありますか。

書：テキストチャット

<8・書く（テキストチャット）>

Text Chat: Graduation

30点
90秒 x 6

You will participate in a simulated exchange of text-chat messages. Each time it is your turn to write, you will have 90 seconds. You should respond as fully and as appropriately as possible.

You will have a conversation about graduation with Takuya Suzuki, a student in Japan.

1. Respond. (90 seconds)

   では、よろしく御願いします。最初の質問です。そちらの卒業式はいつごろどんな所でするんですか。

2. Give a specific response. (90 seconds)

   そうですか。では、次の質問です。卒業生はどんな格好（かっこう）をして、卒業式に参加（さんか）するんですか。

3. Give a reason. (90 seconds)

   ああ、そうですか。では、あなたの学校の卒業式が好きですか。

4. Explain your preference. (90 seconds)

   分かりました。卒業した後の夏休みに、どんなことをしたいですか。

5. Justify your opinion. (90 seconds)

   高校生は卒業をしたら、すぐ大学に進学した方がいいと思いますか。それとも、大学に入る前に一年間休んだ方がいいと思いますか。

6. Ask a specific question. (90 seconds)

   有難うございました。ところで、日本の卒業式について何か質問がありますか。

書：テキストチャット

<９・書く（テキストチャット）>

Text Chat: New Year's Day

30点
90秒 x 6

You will participate in a simulated exchange of text-chat messages. Each time it is your turn to write, you will have 90 seconds. You should respond as fully and as appropriately as possible.

You will have a conversation about New Year's Day with Masa Yamano, a student in Japan.

1. Respond. (90 seconds)

   こんにちは。山本です。今日は御協力ありがとうございます。そちらのお正月についていろいろ教えて下さい。

2. Give a specific response. (90 seconds)

   では、まず一番目の質問です。一般的に言って、アメリカ人はお正月にどんなことをして過ごしているんですか。

3. Give a response. (90 seconds)

   ああ、そうですか。アメリカ人はお正月に教会に行ったりするんですか。

4. Give specific examples. (90 seconds)

   そうですか。では、お正月に特別な伝統的な行事とか食べ物があったら、教えて下さい。

5. Give a preference. (90 seconds)

   分かりました。あなたはクリスマスとお正月で、どちらの方が好きですか。

6. Ask a specific question. (90 seconds)

   どうもいろいろ有難うございました。ところで、日本のお正月について、何か質問がありますか。

<10・書く（テキストチャット）>

Text Chat: Weather

30点
90秒 x 6

You will participate in a simulated exchange of text-chat messages. Each time it is your turn to write, you will have 90 seconds. You should respond as fully and as appropriately as possible.

You will have a conversation about the weather in your hometown with Eriko, your host sister in Japan who is visiting you.

1. Respond. (90 seconds)

   お久しぶり。お元気ですか。私は友達とそちらに来週５日間旅行で行きます。ちょっといろいろ教えて下さい。

2. Give a specific response. (90 seconds)

   そちらのお天気はどうですか。温度は何度ぐらいですか。

3. Give a response. (90 seconds)

   そうですか。私達が行く来週は、雨が降ったりしそうですか。傘（かさ）がいるかしら？

4. Describe a specific example. (90 seconds)

   あ、そうですか。どんな服を持って行ったらいいか分からないんだけど、教えて下さい。

5. Give a specific request. (90 seconds)

   ところで、何か日本からの御土産でほしい物があったら、遠慮（えんりょ）しないで言って下さい。

6. Ask a specific question. (90 seconds)

   いろいろ教えてくれてありがとう。何か質問があったら聞いて下さい。

書：テキストチャット

<11・書く（テキストチャット）>
Text Chat: Cooking

30点
90秒 x 6

You will participate in a simulated exchange of text-chat messages. Each time it is your turn to write, you will have 90 seconds. You should respond as fully and as appropriately as possible.

You will have a conversation about cooking with Kumi Minami, your host mother in Japan.

1. Respond. (90 seconds)

   初めまして。南です。あなたがこの夏、日本に来る時、私達があなたのホストファミリーだそうです。どうぞよろしく。ちょっと質問してもいいですか。

2. Give a specific example. (90 seconds)

   朝晩、私達家族と一緒に食事をすることになるわけなんだけど、何か食べられない物とか嫌いな物とかあったら、教えて下さい。

3. Give a preference. (90 seconds)

   分かりました。それから、和食と洋食とどちらの方が好きですか。

4. Give a specific response. (90 seconds)

   そうですか。うちでは一般的にどんな料理を食べているんですか。からい物でも平気ですか。

5. Describe a specific example. (90 seconds)

   分かりました。ところで、うちで自分で料理したりしますか。何か料理を作ることが出来ますか。

6. Ask a specific question. (90 seconds)

   いろいろありがとう。ところで、私達ホストファミリーに何か質問とかありますか。

<12・書く（テキストチャット）>

Text Chat: Shopping

30点
90秒 x 6

You will participate in a simulated exchange of text-chat messages. Each time it is your turn to write, you will have 90 seconds. You should respond as fully and as appropriately as possible.

You will have a conversation about shopping with Sakura, a student in Japan.

1. Respond. (90 seconds)

   さくらです。よろしくお願いします。質問に答えて下さい。買物が好きですか。

2. Give a specific example. (90 seconds)

   そうですか。今一番買いたい物は何か教えて下さい。どんな物ですか。

3. Give a preference. (90 seconds)

   ああ、そうですか。ところで、ネットで買物をするのと、お店に行って買物をするのと、どちらの方が好きですか。

4. Justify your opinion. (90 seconds)

   そうですか。ネットで買物するのは安全だと思いますか。

5. Give a specific example. (90 seconds)

   分かりました。ところで、もし、あなたが千ドルもらったら、何に使いたいですか。

6. Ask a specific question. (90 seconds)

   有難うございました。何か日本の買物について質問があったら、して下さい。

書：テキストチャット

<13・書く（テキストチャット）>

Text Chat: Japan and the World

30点
90秒 x 6

You will participate in a simulated exchange of text-chat messages. Each time it is your turn to write, you will have 90 seconds. You should respond as fully and as appropriately as possible.

You will have a conversation about Japan with Kenta, a student in Japan.

1. Respond. (90 seconds)

   健太です。どうぞよろしく。日本についてのあなたの率直（そっちょく）な意見を聞かせて下さい。日本が好きですか。

2. Give a specific response. (90 seconds)

   そうですか。現代日本であなたにとって一番興味のあることは何ですか。

3. Give a specific response. (90 seconds)

   ああ、そうですか。ところで、歴史の中で、日米の一番不幸な出来事は何だったと思いますか。

4. Justify your opinion. (90 seconds)

   ちょっと難しい問題ですが、日本とアメリカが仲良くするためには、私達はどんなことをすべきだと思いますか。

5. Give a specific example. (90 seconds)

   将来も日本語の勉強を続けますか。日本語を使って、何をしたいと考えていますか。

6. Ask a specific question. (90 seconds)

   貴重な意見を有難うございました。日本について私に何か質問がありますか。

書：テキストチャット

<書く Compare & Contrast アドバイス>

【Knowledge/skills】
・ Presentational communication
・ Comparing; contrasting; describing; justifying an opinion

【Format】
・ 1 question, 15 points, 20 minutes
・ Written article, 300 - 400 characters

【Speech style】
Use です/ます form or だ form consistently.

【Outline sample structure】
1. Opening:

    これから、AとBをくらべてみます。AとBは違うことも同じこともあります。

2. Three similarities and/or differences between A and B:

    まず 一つ目の違うことは、Aは〜ですが、Bは〜です。

    二つ目の違うことは、〜。

    そして、三つ目の違うことは、〜。

    or しかし、一つの同じことは、AもBも〜。

3. Your preference and reasons:

    （結論（けつろん）として）私はAの方がBより好きです。

    なぜなら、(reason) からです。

【Comparative patterns】
1. Between A and B, I like A more than B. AとBで、Aの方がBより好きです。
2. I don't like B as much as A. BはAほど好きではありません。
3. It's faster to go by car than to walk. 車で行く方が、歩くより速いです。
4. Walking is not as fast as going by car. 歩くのは、車で行くほど速くないです。

【Suggestion】
1. First, plan your outline.
2. Use the AP *kanji*.
3. Proofread well, especially for *kanji*. Check that you have not chosen the wrong *kanji*.

＜１・書く（比較と対比）＞

15点
20分

Compare and Contrast: Family and Friends

Directions: You are writing an article for the student newspaper of your sister school in Japan. Write an article in which you compare and contrast similarities and differences between family and friends. Based on your personal experience, describe at least THREE aspects of each and highlight the similarities and differences between family and friends. Also state your preference for either and give reasons for it.

Your article should be 300 to 400 characters or longer. Use the *desu/masu* or *da* (plain) style, but use one style consistently. Also, use *kanji* wherever *kanji* from the AP Japanese *kanji* list is appropriate. You have 20 minutes to write.

【NOTES/OUTLINE: 自分の作文のアウトラインを書こう！】

Introduction:
_____

Three similarities and differences:

　　1. _____
　　2. _____
　　3. _____

Your preference and give reasons:

_____
_____

書：比較と対比

＜２・書く（比較と対比）＞

15点
20分

Compare and Contrast: Learning Japanese and Learning Another Subject

Directions: You are writing an article for the student newspaper of your sister school in Japan. Write an article in which you compare and contrast learning Japanese and learning another subject of your choice. Based on your personal experience, describe at least THREE aspects of each and highlight the similarities and differences between learning Japanese and learning another subject. Also state your preference and give reasons for it.

Your article should be 300 to 400 characters or longer. Use the *desu/masu* or *da* (plain) style, but use one style consistently. Also, use *kanji* wherever *kanji* from the AP Japanese *kanji* list is appropriate. You have 20 minutes to write.

【NOTES/OUTLINE: 自分の作文のアウトラインを書こう！】

Introduction:
_____

Three similarities and differences:

1. _____
2. _____
3. _____

Your preference and give reasons:

_____
_____

書：比較と対比

<3・書く（比較と対比）>

15点
20分

Compare and Contrast: Weekday Routine and Weekend Routine

Directions: You are writing an article for the student newspaper about your sister school in Japan. Write an article in which you compare and contrast your weekday routine and your weekend routine. Based on your personal life, describe at least THREE differences between your weekday routine and your weekend routine. Also state your preference and give reasons for it.

Your article should be 300 to 400 characters or longer. Use the *desu/masu* or *da* (plain) style, but use one style consistently. Also, use *kanji* wherever *kanji* from the AP Japanese *kanji* list is appropriate. You have 20 minutes to write.

【NOTES/OUTLINE: 自分の作文のアウトラインを書こう！】

Introduction:
_____

Three similarities and differences:

   1. _____
   2. _____
   3. _____

Your preference and give reasons:
_____
_____

[書：比較と対比]

＜４・書く（比較と対比）＞

15点
20分

Compare and Contrast: Music and Sports

Directions: You are writing an article for the student newspaper of your sister school in Japan. Write an article in which you compare and contrast similarities and differences between music and sports. Based on your personal experience, describe at least THREE aspects of each and highlight the similarities and differences between music and sports. Also state your preference for either and give reasons for it.

Your article should be 300 to 400 characters or longer. Use the *desu/masu* or *da* (plain) style, but use one style consistently. Also, use *kanji* wherever *kanji* from the AP Japanese *kanji* list is appropriate. You have 20 minutes to write.

【NOTES/OUTLINE: 自分の作文のアウトラインを書こう！】

Introduction:
_____

Three similarities and differences:

1. _____
2. _____
3. _____

Your preference and give reasons:

_____
_____

書：比較と対比

＜５・書く（比較と対比）＞

15点
20分

Compare and Contrast: Japanese Homes and American Homes

Directions: You are writing an article for the student newspaper of your sister school in Japan. Write an article in which you compare and contrast homes in Japan and the U.S. Based on your personal experience, describe at least THREE aspects of each and highlight the similarities and differences between Japanese homes and American homes. Also state your opinion and give reasons for it.

Your article should be 300 to 400 characters or longer. Use the *desu/masu* or *da* (plain) style, but use one style consistently. Also, use *kanji* wherever *kanji* from the AP Japanese *kanji* list is appropriate. You have 20 minutes to write.

【NOTES/OUTLINE: 自分の作文のアウトラインを書こう！】

Introduction:
_____

Three similarities and differences:

   1. _____
   2. _____
   3. _____

Your preference and give reasons:
_____
_____

書：比較と対比

＜6・書く（比較と対比）＞

15点
20分

Compare and Contrast: Earthquakes and Typhoons

Directions: You are writing an article for the student newspaper of your sister school in Japan. Write an article in which you compare and contrast earthquakes and typhoons. Based on your personal experience, describe at least THREE aspects of each and highlight the similarities and differences between earthquakes and typhoons. Also state your opinion and give reasons for it.

Your article should be 300 to 400 characters or longer. Use the *desu/masu* or *da* (plain) style, but use one style consistently. Also, use *kanji* wherever *kanji* from the AP Japanese *kanji* list is appropriate. You have 20 minutes to write.

【NOTES/OUTLINE: 自分の作文のアウトラインを書こう！】

Introduction:
_____

Three similarities and differences:

 1. _____
 2. _____
 3. _____

Your opinion and give reasons:
_____
_____

書：比較と対比

<7・書く（比較と対比）>

15点
20分

Compare and Contrast: Japanese Kimono and Western Clothes

Directions: You are writing an article for the student newspaper of your sister school in Japan. Write an article in which you compare and contrast Japanese *kimono* and Western clothes. Based on your personal experience, describe at least THREE aspects of each and highlight the similarities and differences between Japanese *kimono* and Western clothes. Also state your opinion and give reasons for it.

Your article should be 300 to 400 characters or longer. Use the *desu/masu* or *da* (plain) style, but use one style consistently. Also, use *kanji* wherever *kanji* from the AP Japanese *kanji* list is appropriate. You have 20 minutes to write.

【NOTES/OUTLINE: 自分の作文のアウトラインを書こう！】

Introduction:
_____

Three similarities and differences:

1. _____
2. _____
3. _____

Your preference and give reasons:
_____
_____

書：比較と対比

＜8・書く（比較と対比）＞

15点
20分

Compare and Contrast: Watching Movies at a Movie Theater and Watching DVDs at Home

Directions: You are writing an article for the student newspaper of your sister school in Japan. Write an article in which you compare and contrast watching movies at a movie theater and watching DVDs at home. Based on your personal experience, describe at least THREE aspects of each and highlight the similarities and differences between a movie theater and DVD rental. Also state your preference and give reasons for it.

Your article should be 300 to 400 characters or longer. Use the *desu/masu* or *da* (plain) style, but use one style consistently. Also, use *kanji* wherever *kanji* from the AP Japanese *kanji* list is appropriate. You have 20 minutes to write.

【NOTES/OUTLINE: 自分の作文のアウトラインを書こう！】

Introduction:
_____

Three similarities and differences:

1. _____
2. _____
3. _____

Your preference and give reasons:
_____
_____

書：比較と対比

＜9・書く（比較と対比）＞

15点
20分

Compare and Contrast: Cellular phones and E-mail

Directions: You are writing an article for the student newspaper of your sister school in Japan. Write an article in which you compare and contrast the use of cellular phones and e-mail. Based on your personal experience, describe at least THREE aspects of each and highlight the similarities and differences between using cellular phones and e-mail. Also state your opinion and give reasons for it.

Your article should be 300 to 400 characters or longer. Use the *desu/masu* or *da* (plain) style, but use one style consistently. Also, use *kanji* wherever *kanji* from the AP Japanese *kanji* list is appropriate. You have 20 minutes to write.

【NOTES/OUTLINE: 自分の作文のアウトラインを書こう！】

Introduction: _____

Three similarities and differences:

1. _____
2. _____
3. _____

Your preference and give reasons: _____
_____

書：比較と対比

＜10・書く（比較と対比）＞

15点
20分

Compare and Contrast: Waiters and Store Clerks

Directions: You are writing an article for the student newspaper of your sister school in Japan. Write an article in which you compare and contrast working as a waiter and as a store clerk. Based on your personal experience, describe at least THREE aspects of each and highlight the similarities and differences between working as a waiter and as a store cleark. Also state your preference and give reasons for it.

Your article should be 300 to 400 characters or longer. Use the *desu/masu* or *da* (plain) style, but use one style consistently. Also, use *kanji* wherever *kanji* from the AP Japanese *kanji* list is appropriate. You have 20 minutes to write.

【NOTES/OUTLINE: 自分の作文のアウトラインを書こう！】

Introduction:
___

Three similarities and differences:

1. ___
2. ___
3. ___

Your preference and give reasons:
___
___

書：比較と対比

<11・書く（比較と対比）>

15点
20分

Compare and Contrast: Proms and Weddings

Directions: You are writing an article for the student newspaper of your sister school in Japan. Write an article in which you compare and contrast aspects of proms and weddings in America. Based on your personal experience, describe at least THREE aspects of each and highlight the similarities and differences between aspects of proms and weddings in America. Also state your opinion and give reasons for it.

Your article should be 300 to 400 characters or longer. Use the *desu/masu* or *da* (plain) style, but use one style consistently. Also, use *kanji* wherever *kanji* from the AP Japanese *kanji* list is appropriate. You have 20 minutes to write.

【NOTES/OUTLINE: 自分の作文のアウトラインを書こう！】

Introduction:
_____

Three similarities and differences:

1. _____
2. _____
3. _____

Your opinion and give reasons:
_____
_____

書：比較と対比

<12・書く（比較と対比）>

15点
20分

Compare and Contrast: Subways and Cars

Directions: You are writing an article for the student newspaper of your sister school in Japan. Write an article in which you compare and contrast using subways and cars. Based on your personal experience, describe at least THREE aspects of each and highlight the similarities and differences between these methods of transportation. Also state your preference and give reasons for it.

Your article should be 300 to 400 characters or longer. Use the *desu/masu* or *da* (plain) style, but use one style consistently. Also, use *kanji* wherever *kanji* from the AP Japanese *kanji* list is appropriate. You have 20 minutes to write.

【NOTES/OUTLINE: 自分の作文のアウトラインを書こう！】

Introduction:
_____

Three similarities and differences:

1. _____
2. _____
3. _____

Your preference and give reasons:
_____
_____

書：比較と対比

<13・書く（比較と対比）>

15点
20分

Compare and Contrast:
  Japanese Department Stores and American Department Stores

Directions: You are writing an article for the student newspaper of your sister school in Japan. Write an article in which you compare and contrast department stores in Japan and the U.S. Based on your personal experience, describe at least THREE aspects of each and highlight the similarities and differences between department stores in Japan and the U.S. Also state your preference and give reasons for it.

Your article should be 300 to 400 characters or longer. Use the *desu/masu* or *da* (plain) style, but use one style consistently. Also, use *kanji* wherever *kanji* from the AP Japanese *kanji* list is appropriate. You have 20 minutes to write.

【NOTES/OUTLINE: 自分の作文のアウトラインを書こう！】

Introduction:
_____

Three similarities and differences:

  1. _____
  2. _____
  3. _____

Your preference and give reasons:
_____
_____

書：比較と対比

<14・書く（比較と対比）>

15点
20分

Compare and Contrast: A Healthy Lifestyle and an Unhealthy Lifestyle

Directions: You are writing an article for the student newspaper of your sister school in Japan. Write an article in which you compare and contrast a healthy lifestyle and an unhealthy lifestyle. Based on your personal experience, describe at least THREE similarities and differences between a healthy lifestyle and an unhealthy lifestyle. Also state your preference and give reasons for it.

Your article should be 300 to 400 characters or longer. Use the *desu/masu* or *da* (plain) style, but use one style consistently. Also, use *kanji* wherever *kanji* from the AP Japanese *kanji* list is appropriate. You have 20 minutes to write.

【NOTES/OUTLINE: 自分の作文のアウトラインを書こう！】

Introduction:
_____

Three similarities and differences:

1. _____
2. _____
3. _____

Your preference and give reasons:
_____
_____

書：比較と対比

<15・書く（比較と対比）>

15点
20分

Compare and Contrast: Traveling by Airplane and Traveling by Car

Directions: You are writing an article for the student newspaper of your sister school in Japan. Write an article in which you compare and contrast traveling by airplane and traveling by car. Based on your personal experience, describe at least THREE similarities and differences between traveling by airplane and traveling by car. Also state your preference and give reasons for it.

Your article should be 300 to 400 characters or longer. Use the *desu/masu* or *da* (plain) style, but use one style consistently. Also, use *kanji* wherever *kanji* from the AP Japanese *kanji* list is appropriate. You have 20 minutes to write.

【NOTES/OUTLINE: 自分の作文のアウトラインを書こう！】

Introduction:
_____

Three similarities and differences:

1. _____
2. _____
3. _____

Your preference and give reasons:
_____
_____

書：比較と対比

<書く Cultural Topic Posting アドバイス>

【Knowledge/skills】
- Presentational communication
- Describing and expressing opinions about a Japanese cultural practice or product

【Format】
- 1 question, 15 points, 20 minutes
- Written article, 300 - 400 characters

【Speech style】
Use です/ます form or だ form consistently.

【Outline sample structure】
1. Introduction:
   これから、〜について述(の)べたいと思います。
2. One example:
   (Topic) の中にいろいろありますが、私は (one example) について、述(の)べたいと思います。
3. Three characteristics of the example:
   まず (or 最初に or 一番目に)、
   次に (or 二番目に)、
   そして、最後に (or 三番目に)、
4. Your opinion and feelings:
   結論(けつろん)として、私は〜と思います。

【Suggestion】
1. First, plan your outline.
2. Use the AP *kanji*.
3. Proofread well, especially for *kanji*.

＜１・書く（文化）＞

15点
20分

Cultural Topic Posting: Japanese Family Member's Role

You are responding to a posting in a Web forum for high school students of Japanese. The posting asks about Japanese family members' roles. Select ONE example of a Japanese family member, such as the father, mother, eldest son, etc. Describe in detail at least THREE characteristics of the family member you choose. Also, express your opinion or feelings about the family member's role.

Your article should be 300 to 400 characters or longer. Use the *desu/masu* or *da* (plain) style, but use one style consistently. Also, use *kanji* wherever *kanji* from the AP Japanese *kanji* list is appropriate. You have 20 minutes to write.

【NOTES/OUTLINE: 自分の作文のアウトラインを書こう！】

Introduction:
_____

One example:
_____

Three characteristics of the example:

1. _____
2. _____
3. _____

Your opinion or feelings:
_____
_____

書：文化

＜２・書く（文化）＞

15点
20分

Cultural Topic Posting: Religions in Japan

You are responding to a posting in a Web forum for high school students of Japanese. The posting asks about religions in Japan. Select ONE example of a Japanese religion, such as Shinto, Buddhism, etc. Describe in detail at least THREE characteristics of the Japanese religion. Also, express your opinion or feelings about the Japanese religion.

Your article should be 300 to 400 characters or longer. Use the *desu/masu* or *da* (plain) style, but use one style consistently. Also, use *kanji* wherever *kanji* from the AP Japanese *kanji* list is appropriate. You have 20 minutes to write.

【NOTES/OUTLINE: 自分の作文のアウトラインを書こう！】

Introduction:
_____

One example:
_____

Three characteristics of the example:

1. _____
2. _____
3. _____

Your opinion or feelings:
_____
_____

書：文化

<3・書く（文化）>

15点
20分

Cultural Topic Posting: Famous Japanese Cities

You are responding to a posting in a Web forum for high school students of Japanese. The posting asks about famous cities in Japan. Select ONE example of a famous Japanese city, such as Tokyo, Kyoto, Nara, Sapporo, Hiroshima, Fukuoka, etc. Describe in detail at least THREE characteristics of the city. Also, express your opinion or feelings about the city.

Your article should be 300 to 400 characters or longer. Use the *desu/masu* or *da* (plain) style, but use one style consistently. Also, use *kanji* wherever *kanji* from the AP Japanese *kanji* list is appropriate. You have 20 minutes to write.

【NOTES/OUTLINE: 自分の作文のアウトラインを書こう！】

Introduction:
_____

One example:
_____

Three characteristics of the example:

1. _____
2. _____
3. _____

Your opinion or feelings:
_____
_____

書：文化

＜４・書く（文化）＞

15点
20分

Cultural Topic Posting: Natural Disasters in Japan

You are responding to a posting in a Web forum for high school students of Japanese. The posting asks about natural disasters in Japan. Select ONE example of a natural disaster in Japan, such as typhoons, earthquakes, tsunami, volucano eruptions, etc. Describe in detail at least THREE characteristics of the natural disaster. Also, express your opinion or feelings about the natural disaster.

Your article should be 300 to 400 characters or longer. Use the *desu/masu* or *da* (plain) style, but use one style consistently. Also, use *kanji* wherever *kanji* from the AP Japanese *kanji* list is appropriate. You have 20 minutes to write.

【NOTES/OUTLINE: 自分の作文のアウトラインを書こう！】

Introduction:
_____

One example:
_____

Three characteristics of the example:

  1. _____
  2. _____
  3. _____

Your opinion or feelings:
_____
_____

＜5・書く（文化）＞

15点
20分

Cultural Topic Posting: Japanese School Event

You are responding to a posting in a Web forum for high school students of Japanese. The posting asks about annual events in Japan. Select ONE example of a Japanese school event, such as a graduation ceremony, entrance ceremony, school athletic meet, cultural festival, excursion, etc. Describe in detail at least THREE characteristics of the school event. Also, express your opinion or feelings about the event.

Your article should be 300 to 400 characters or longer. Use the *desu/masu* or *da* (plain) style, but use one style consistently. Also, use *kanji* wherever *kanji* from the AP Japanese *kanji* list is appropriate. You have 20 minutes to write.

【NOTES/OUTLINE: 自分の作文のアウトラインを書こう！】

Introduction:
_____

One example:
_____

Three characteristics of the example:

1. _____
2. _____
3. _____

Your opinion or feelings:
_____
_____

書：文化

＜6・書く（文化）＞

15点 20分

Cultural Topic Posting: Japanese TV Programs

You are responding to a posting in a Web forum for high school students of Japanese. The posting asks about Japanese TV programs. Select ONE example of a category of Japanese TV programs, such as TV dramas, singing programs, cartoons (anime), etc. Describe in detail at least THREE characteristics of this type of TV program. Also, express your opinion or feelings about this type of TV program.

Your article should be 300 to 400 characters or longer. Use the *desu/masu* or *da* (plain) style, but use one style consistently. Also, use *kanji* wherever *kanji* from the AP Japanese *kanji* list is appropriate. You have 20 minutes to write.

【NOTES/OUTLINE: 自分の作文のアウトラインを書こう！】

Introduction:
_____

One example:
_____

Three characteristics of the example:
 1. _____
 2. _____
 3. _____

Your opinion or feelings:
_____
_____

書：文化

＜7・書く（文化）＞

15点
20分

Cultural Topic Posting: Japanese Cars

You are responding to a posting in a Web forum for high school students of Japanese. The posting asks about Japanese cars. Select ONE example of a Japanese car. Describe in detail at least THREE characteristics of the car. Also, express your opinion or feelings about the car.

Your article should be 300 to 400 characters or longer. Use the *desu/masu* or *da* (plain) style, but use one style consistently. Also, use *kanji* wherever *kanji* from the AP Japanese *kanji* list is appropriate. You have 20 minutes to write.

【NOTES/OUTLINE: 自分の作文のアウトラインを書こう！】

Introduction:
_____

One example:
_____

Three characteristics of the example:

1. _____
2. _____
3. _____

Your opinion or feelings:
_____
_____

書：文化

<8・書く（文化）>

15点
20分

Cultural Topic Posting: Japanese Speech Styles

You are responding to a posting in a Web forum for high school students of Japanese. The posting asks about Japanese speech styles. Select ONE example of a Japanese speech style, such as the honorific style, informal style, male/female speech, etc. Describe in detail at least THREE characteristics of the speech style. Also, express your opinion or feelings about the speech style.

Your article should be 300 to 400 characters or longer. Use the *desu/masu* or *da* (plain) style, but use one style consistently. Also, use *kanji* wherever *kanji* from the AP Japanese *kanji* list is appropriate. You have 20 minutes to write.

【NOTES/OUTLINE: 自分の作文のアウトラインを書こう！】

Introduction:
_____

One example:
_____

Three characteristics of the example:

1. _____
2. _____
3. _____

Your opinion or feelings:
_____
_____

書：文化

<9・書く（文化）>

15点
20分

Cultural Topic Posting: Japanese Annual Events

You are responding to a posting in a Web forum for high school students of Japanese. The posting asks about annual events in Japan. Select ONE example of a Japanese annual event, such as New Year's Day, cherry blossom viewing, Children's Day, Star Festival, etc. Describe in detail at least THREE characteristics of the annual event. Also, express your opinion or feelings about the event.

Your article should be 300 to 400 characters or longer. Use the *desu/masu* or *da* (plain) style, but use one style consistently. Also, use kanji wherever kanji from the AP Japanese kanji list is appropriate. You have 20 minutes to write.

【NOTES/OUTLINE: 自分の作文のアウトラインを書こう！】

Introduction:
_____

One example:
_____

Three characteristics of the example:

1. _____
2. _____
3. _____

Your opinion or feelings:
_____
_____

書：文化

<10・書く（文化）>

15点
20分

Cultural Topic Posting: Japanese Seasons

You are responding to a posting in a Web forum for high school students of Japanese. The posting asks about seasons in Japan. Select ONE season; spring, summer, autumn or winter. Describe in detail at least THREE characteristics of the season in Japan. Also, express your opinion or feelings about the season.

Your article should be 300 to 400 characters or longer. Use the *desu/masu* or *da* (plain) style, but use one style consistently. Also, use *kanji* wherever *kanji* from the AP Japanese *kanji* list is appropriate. You have 20 minutes to write.

【NOTES/OUTLINE: 自分の作文のアウトラインを書こう！】

Introduction:
_____

One example:
_____

Three characteristics of the example:

1. _____
2. _____
3. _____

Your opinion or feelings:
_____
_____

書：文化

<11・書く（文化）>

15点
20分

Cultural Topic Posting: Japanese Food

You are responding to a posting in a Web forum for high school students of Japanese. The posting asks about Japanese food. Select ONE example of a Japanese food, such as a box lunch, noodles, sushi, etc. Describe in detail at least THREE characteristics of the Japanese food. Also, express your opinion or feelings about the Japanese food.

Your article should be 300 to 400 characters or longer. Use the *desu/masu* or *da* (plain) style, but use one style consistently. Also, use *kanji* wherever *kanji* from the AP Japanese *kanji* list is appropriate. You have 20 minutes to write.

【NOTES/OUTLINE: 自分の作文のアウトラインを書こう！】

Introduction:
_____

One example:
_____

Three characteristics of the example:

1. _____
2. _____
3. _____

Your opinion or feelings:
_____
_____

<12・書く（文化）>

15点
20分

Cultural Topic Posting: Traditional Japanese Medical Treatments

You are responding to a posting in a Web forum for high school students of Japanese. The posting asks about Japanese treatment. Select ONE example of a traditional Japanese medical treatment, such as *shiatsu* massage, acupuncture, Chinese herbal medicine, etc. Describe in detail at least THREE characteristics of the treatment. Also, express your opinion or feelings about the treatment.

Your article should be 300 to 400 characters or longer. Use the *desu/masu* or *da* (plain) style, but use one style consistently. Also, use *kanji* wherever *kanji* from the AP Japanese *kanji* list is appropriate. You have 20 minutes to write.

【NOTES/OUTLINE: 自分の作文のアウトラインを書こう！】

Introduction:
_____

One example:
_____

Three characteristics of the example:

  1. _____
  2. _____
  3. _____

Your opinion or feelings:
_____
_____

書：文化

<13・書く（文化）>

15点
20分

Cultural Topic Posting: Japanese Folk Tales

You are responding to a posting in a Web forum for high school students of Japanese. The posting asks about Japanese folk tales. Select ONE example of a Japanese folk tale, such as *Momotaro, Kaguyahime, Urashima Taro*, etc. Describe in detail at least THREE characteristics of the folk tale. Also, express your opinion or feelings about the folk tale.

Your article should be 300 to 400 characters or longer. Use the *desu/masu* or *da* (plain) style, but use one style consistently. Also, use *kanji* wherever *kanji* from the AP Japanese *kanji* list is appropriate. You have 20 minutes to write.

【NOTES/OUTLINE: 自分の作文のアウトラインを書こう！】

Introduction:
_____

One example:
_____

Three characteristics of the example:

1. _____
2. _____
3. _____

Your opinion or feelings:
_____
_____

書：文化

<話す Conversation アドバイス>

You can download the audio recordings for this section from http://www.cheng-tsui.com/downloads.

【Knowledge/skills】
- Interpersonal communication
- Participating in conversation by responding appropriately

【Format】
- 4 prompts as part of 1 conversation
- 4 questions x 20 seconds, 15 points, 3 minutes total

【Speech style】
Immediately decide on which speech style you should use, which depends on the person to whom you are speaking.

【Responding appropriately to expressions】
1. 日本人：「ご協力お願いします。」
   答え：「はい、分かりました。何でも聞いて下さい。協力します。」
2. 日本人：「がんばってください。」
   答え：「はい、がんばります。」

【Polite style and informal style】
1. "Let me see..."
   Polite style: そうですねえ。。。
   Informal style (male): そうだねえ。。。
   Informal style (female): そうねえ。。。
2. "have to decide..."
   Polite style: 決めなければなりません
   Informal style: 決めなくちゃ

【Suggestion】
1. Make sure to speak loudly and clearly. Use a confident voice.
2. Begin with a cheerful greeting.
3. After introducing yourself, say どうぞよろしくお願いします。

4. Carry on a polite conversation.
5. At the end, close your conversation with a word of appreciation and a polite closing remark.
   Ex. どうも有難うございました。
6. When you don't know much about the topic asked, you may answer
   「topic についてよく知りませんから、私は答えられません。」
7. 「分かりません」and「もう一度言って下さい」do not count as correct answers.
8. Listen to the questions carefully. If you don't understand the question, repeat back the question. At minimum, say「そうですねえ...」

【Suggestions for improving your listening skills】
1. Practice engaging in impromptu conversations in Japanese.
2. Listen to Japanese radio programs and Japanese songs, watch Japanese TV programs, Japanese movies, anime, etc.

<1・話す（会話）>

15点
20秒 x 4

Conversation: Host Mother

You will participate in a simulated conversation. Each time it is your turn to speak, you will have 20 seconds to record. You should respond as fully and as appropriately as possible.

You will introduce yourself in a conversation with Mrs. Kondo, the mother of your Japanese host family.

(Host mother)

(20 seconds)

(Host mother)

(20 seconds)

(Host mother)

(20 seconds)

(Host mother)

(20 seconds)

＜２・話す（会話）＞

15点
20秒 x 4

Conversation: Sports

You will participate in a simulated conversation. Each time it is your turn to speak, you will have 20 seconds to record. You should respond as fully and as appropriately as possible.

You will introduce yourself in a conversation with Mr. Ito, a newpaper reporter from Japan.

(Male reporter)

(20 seconds)

(Male reporter)

(20 seconds)

(Male reporter)

(20 seconds)

(Male reporter)

(20 seconds)

話：会話

＜3・話す（会話）＞

Conversation: Home

15点
20秒 x 4

You will participate in a simulated conversation. Each time it is your turn to speak, you will have 20 seconds to record. You should respond as fully and as appropriately as possible.

You will have a conversation with Daisuke Kato, a Japanese student who is going to stay in your house.

(Male student)

(20 seconds)

(Male student)

(20 seconds)

(Male student)

(20 seconds)

(Male student)

(20 seconds)

話：会話

<4・話す（会話）>

15点
20秒 x 4

Conversation: Recycling

You will participate in a simulated conversation. Each time it is your turn to speak, you will have 20 seconds to record. You should respond as fully and as appropriately as possible.

You will have a conversation with Dr. Kawano, a professor from a Japanese university.

(Professor)

(20 seconds)

(Professor)

(20 seconds)

(Professor)

(20 seconds)

(Professor)

(20 seconds)

＜５・話す（会話）＞

Conversation: School

15点
20秒 x 4

You will participate in a simulated conversation. Each time it is your turn to speak, you will have 20 seconds to record. You should respond as fully and as appropriately as possible.

You will have a conversation with Mr. Yamamura, the father of your Japanese host family.

(Host father)

(20 seconds)

(Host father)

(20 seconds)

(Host father)

(20 seconds)

(Host father)

(20 seconds)

<6・話す（会話）>

Conversation: Fashion

15点
20秒 x 4

You will participate in a simulated conversation. Each time it is your turn to speak, you will have 20 seconds to record. You should respond as fully and as appropriately as possible.

You will have a telephone conversation with Mai, a Japanese student.

(Female Student)

(20 seconds)

(Female Student)

(20 seconds)

(Female Student)

(20 seconds)

(Female Student)

(20 seconds)

<7・話す（会話）>

15点
20秒 x 4

Conversation: Cellular Phones

You will participate in a simulated conversation. Each time it is your turn to speak, you will have 20 seconds to record. You should respond as fully and as appropriately as possible.

You will have a conversation with Kyoko, a student from Japan.

(Student)

(20 seconds)

(Student)

(20 seconds)

(Student)

(20 seconds)

(Student)

(20 seconds)

<8・話す（会話）>

Conversation: Job

15点
20秒 x 4

You will participate in a simulated conversation. Each time it is your turn to speak, you will have 20 seconds to record. You should respond as fully and as appropriately as possible.

You will have a conversation with Mrs. Nakata, an interviewer from a Japanese radio station.

(Interviewer)

(20 seconds)

(Interviewer)

(20 seconds)

(Interviewer)

(20 seconds)

(Interviewer)

(20 seconds)

＜9・話す（会話）＞

15点
20秒 x 4

Conversation: Christmas

You will participate in a simulated conversation. Each time it is your turn to speak, you will have 20 seconds to record. You should respond as fully and as appropriately as possible.

You will have a conversation with Mrs. Nakamura, the mother of your Japanese host family.

(Host mother)

(20 seconds)

(Host mother)

(20 seconds)

(Host mother)

(20 seconds)

(Host mother)

(20 seconds)

話：会話

<10・話す（会話）>

15点
20秒 x 4

Conversation: Commuting to School

You will participate in a simulated conversation. Each time it is your turn to speak, you will have 20 seconds to record. You should respond as fully and as appropriately as possible.

You will have a conversation with Mr. Nakamura, a Japanese school newspaper writer, about commuting to school.

(Man)

(20 seconds)

(Man)

(20 seconds)

(Man)

(20 seconds)

(Man)

(20 seconds)

<11・話す（会話）>

15点
20秒 x 4

Conversation: Souvenir Shopping

You will participate in a simulated conversation. Each time it is your turn to speak, you will have 20 seconds to record. You should respond as fully and as appropriately as possible.

You will have a conversation with a Japanese customer at the souvenir shop where you are working.

(Customer)

(20 seconds)

(Customer)

(20 seconds)

(Customer)

(20 seconds)

(Customer)

(20 seconds)

<12・話す（会話）>

15点
20秒x4

Conversation: An Injury

You will participate in a simulated conversation. Each time it is your turn to speak, you will have 20 seconds to record. You should respond as fully and as appropriately as possible.

You have fractured your arm in Japan and you will have a conversation with Mr. Tsuda, a Japanese teacher at your Japanese host school.

(Teacher)

(20 seconds)

(Teacher)

(20 seconds)

(Teacher)

(20 seconds)

(Teacher)

(20 seconds)

<13・話す（会話）>

Conversation: Japan Trip

15点
20秒 x 4

You will participate in a simulated conversation. Each time it is your turn to speak, you will have 20 seconds to record. You should respond as fully and as appropriately as possible.

You will have a conversation with Mr. Okada, a Japanese visitor at your school.

(Visitor)

(20 seconds)

(Visitor)

(20 seconds)

(Visitor)

(20 seconds)

(Visitor)

(20 seconds)

<話す Return Telephone Call アドバイス>

You can download the audio recordings for this section from http://www.cheng-tsui.com/downloads.

【Knowledge/skills】
- Interpersonal communication
- Participating in a conversation by responding appropriately

【Format】
- 4 prompts in 1 telephone call
- 4 questions X 20 seconds, 15 points, 3 minutes total

【Speech style】
Immediately decide on which speech style you will use, which should depend on the person to whom you are speaking.

【Sample structure】
1. After listening to the telephone message:
    [Polite form]
    もしもし、(your last name) です。留守番電話を聞きましたが、_____
    (Repeat the message) そうですね。[Respond with your reaction to the situation.]
    [Informal form]
    もしもし、(your first name) だけど。留守番電話を聞いたけど、_____
    (Repeat the message) だって。[Respond with your reaction to the situation.]

【Helpful Expressions】
1. When congratulating someone, say:
    [Polite form] おめでとうございます。[Informal form] おめでとう。
2. When you hear good news, say:
    [Polite form] それは良かったですねえ。[Informal form] それは良かったねえ。
3. When you hear disappointing news, say:
    [Polite form] それは残念でしたねえ。[Informal form] それは残念だったねえ。
4. When you hear about some physical problem, say:
    [Polite form] 大丈夫ですか。[Informal form] 大丈夫？

5. When you hear about sad news such as death or a serious illness, say:
   [Polite form] お気のどくに。 [Informal form] 気のどくに。
6. When you want to express pity, say:
   [Polite form] Not applicable. [Informal form] かわいそう。

【Suggestions】
1. Make sure to speak loudly and clearly. Use a confident voice.
2. Begin with a cheerful greeting.
3. After introducing yourself, say どうぞよろしくお願いします。
4. Carry on a polite conversation.
5. At the end, close your talk with a word of appreciation and an appropriate remark.

[Polite form]	[Informal form]
どうも有難うございました。	どうも有難う。
では、また。	じゃ、またね。
また後で電話します。	また後で電話するね。
失礼します。	じゃね。

＜１・話す（留守番電話）＞

15点
20秒 x 4

Return Telephone Call: Welcome Party

You will participate in a simulated telephone conversation with someone you are calling back after receiving a message. First, you will listen to the voice message. Then the telephone call will begin. Each time it is your turn to speak, you will have 20 seconds to record. You should respond as fully and as appropriately as possible.

(Narrator)   Listen to the voice message.

(Woman)

(Narrator)   Now the telephone call will begin. After the phone is answered, begin with a greeting and then explain why you are calling.

(Woman)   [Telephone] [Rings twice and picks up]

(20 seconds)

(Woman)

(20 seconds)

(Woman)

(20 seconds)

(Woman)

(20 seconds)

<2・話す（留守番電話）>

15点
20秒×4

Return Telephone Call: Breaking a Date

You will participate in a simulated telephone conversation with someone you are calling back after receiving a message. First, you will listen to the voice message. Then the telephone call will begin. Each time it is your turn to speak, you will have 20 seconds to record. You should respond as fully and as appropriately as possible.

(Narrator)   Listen to the voice message.

(Woman)

(Narrator)   Now the telephone call will begin. After the phone is answered, begin with a greeting and then explain why you are calling.

(Woman)   [Telephone] [Rings twice and picks up]

(20 seconds)

(Woman)

(20 seconds)

(Woman)

(20 seconds)

(Woman)

(20 seconds)

話：留守番電話

＜3・話す（留守番電話）＞

15点 20秒 x 4

Return Telephone Call: Karaoke

You will participate in a simulated telephone conversation with someone you are calling back after receiving a message. First, you will listen to the voice message. Then the telephone call will begin. Each time it is your turn to speak, you will have 20 seconds to record. You should respond as fully and as appropriately as possible.

(Narrator)   Listen to the voice message.

(Woman)

(Narrator)   Now the telephone call will begin. After the phone is answered, begin with a greeting and then explain why you are calling.

(Woman)   [Telephone] [Rings twice and picks up]

(20 seconds)

(Woman)

(20 seconds)

(Woman)

(20 seconds)

(Woman)

(20 seconds)

＜４・話す（留守番電話）＞

Return Telephone Call: Community Service

15点
20秒 x 4

You will participate in a simulated telephone conversation with someone you are calling back after receiving a message. First, you will listen to the voice message. Then the telephone call will begin. Each time it is your turn to speak, you will have 20 seconds to record. You should respond as fully and as appropriately as possible.

(Narrator)   Listen to the voice message.

(Woman)

(Narrator)   Now the telephone call will begin. After the phone is answered, begin with a greeting and then explain why you are calling.

(Woman)   [Telephone] [Rings twice and picks up]

(20 seconds)

(Woman)

(20 seconds)

(Woman)

(20 seconds)

(Woman)

(20 seconds)

<5・話す（留守番電話）>

15点
20秒 x 4

Return Telephone Call: College Decisions

You will participate in a simulated telephone conversation with someone you are calling back after receiving a message. First, you will listen to the voice message. Then the telephone call will begin. Each time it is your turn to speak, you will have 20 seconds to record. You should respond as fully and as appropriately as possible.

(Narrator)   Listen to the voice message.

(Man)

(Narrator)   Now the telephone call will begin. After the phone is answered, begin with a greeting and then explain why you are calling.

(Man)   [Telephone] [Rings twice and picks up]

(20 seconds)

(Man)

(20 seconds)

(Man)

(20 seconds)

(Man)

(20 seconds)

<6・話す（留守番電話）>

15点
20秒 x 4

Return Telephone Call: Dance Party

You will participate in a simulated telephone conversation with someone you are calling back after receiving a message. First, you will listen to the voice message. Then the telephone call will begin. Each time it is your turn to speak, you will have 20 seconds to record. You should respond as fully and as appropriately as possible.

(Narrator)　　Listen to the voice message.

(Girl)

(Narrator)　　Now the telephone call will begin. After the phone is answered, begin with a greeting and then explain why you are calling.

(Girl)　　[Telephone] [Rings twice and picks up]

(20 seconds)

(Girl)

(20 seconds)

(Girl)

(20 seconds)

(Girl)

(20 seconds)

＜7・話す（留守番電話）＞

Return Telephone Call: Cellular Phone

15点
20秒 x 4

You will participate in a simulated telephone conversation with someone you are calling back after receiving a message. First, you will listen to the voice message. Then the telephone call will begin. Each time it is your turn to speak, you will have 20 seconds to record. You should respond as fully and as appropriately as possible.

(Narrator)　　Listen to the voice message.

(Man)

(Narrator)　　Now the telephone call will begin. After the phone is answered, begin with a greeting and then explain why you are calling.

(Man)　　[Telephone] [Rings twice and picks up]

(20 seconds)

(Man)

(20 seconds)

(Man)

(20 seconds)

(Man)

(20 seconds)

<8・話す（留守番電話）>

15点
20秒 x 4

Return Telephone Call: Speech

You will participate in a simulated telephone conversation with someone you are calling back after receiving a message. First, you will listen to the voice message. Then the telephone call will begin. Each time it is your turn to speak, you will have 20 seconds to record. You should respond as fully and as appropriately as possible.

(Narrator)   Listen to the voice message.

(Woman)

(Narrator)   Now the telephone call will begin. After the phone is answered, begin with a greeting and then explain why you are calling.

(Woman)   [Telephone] [Rings twice and picks up]

(20 seconds)

(Woman)

(20 seconds)

(Woman)

(20 seconds)

(Woman)

(20 seconds)

話：留守番電話

<9・話す（留守番電話）>

15点
20秒 x 4

Return Telephone Call: Christmas Cake

You will participate in a simulated telephone conversation with someone you are calling back after receiving a message. First, you will listen to the voice message. Then the telephone call will begin. Each time it is your turn to speak, you will have 20 seconds to record. You should respond as fully and as appropriately as possible.

(Narrator)　　Listen to the voice message.

(Woman)

(Narrator)　　Now the telephone call will begin. After the phone is answered, begin with a greeting and then explain why you are calling.

(Woman)　　[Telephone] [Rings twice and picks up]

(20 seconds)

(Woman)

(20 seconds)

(Woman)

(20 seconds)

(Woman)

(20 seconds)

話：留守番電話

<10・話す（留守番電話）>

Return Telephone Call: Hiking

15点
20秒 x 4

You will participate in a simulated telephone conversation with someone you are calling back after receiving a message. First, you will listen to the voice message. Then the telephone call will begin. Each time it is your turn to speak, you will have 20 seconds to record. You should respond as fully and as appropriately as possible.

(Narrator)　　Listen to the voice message.

(Man)

(Narrator)　　Now the telephone call will begin. After the phone is answered, begin with a greeting and then explain why you are calling.

(Man)　　　　[Telephone] [Rings twice and picks up]

(20 seconds)

(Man)

(20 seconds)

(Man)

(20 seconds)

(Man)

(20 seconds)

話：留守番電話

<11・話す（留守番電話）>

Return Telephone Call: Pizza

15点
20秒 x 4

You will participate in a simulated telephone conversation with someone you are calling back after receiving a message. First, you will listen to the voice message. Then the telephone call will begin. Each time it is your turn to speak, you will have 20 seconds to record. You should respond as fully and as appropriately as possible.

(Narrator)   Listen to the voice message.

(Man)

(Narrator)   Now the telephone call will begin. After the phone is answered, begin with a greeting and then explain why you are calling.

(Man)   [Telephone] [Rings twice and picks up]

(20 seconds)

(Man)

(20 seconds)

(Man)

(20 seconds)

(Man)

(20 seconds)

話：留守番電話

<12・話す（留守番電話）>

15点
20秒 x 4

Return Telephone Call: Department Store

You will participate in a simulated telephone conversation with someone you are calling back after receiving a message. First, you will listen to the voice message. Then the telephone call will begin. Each time it is your turn to speak, you will have 20 seconds to record. You should respond as fully and as appropriately as possible.

(Narrator)   Listen to the voice message.

(Woman)

(Narrator)   Now the telephone call will begin. After the phone is answered, begin with a greeting and then explain why you are calling.

(Woman)   [Telephone] [Rings twice and picks up]

(20 seconds)

(Woman)

(20 seconds)

(Woman)

(20 seconds)

(Woman)

(20 seconds)

<13・話す（留守番電話）>

15点
20秒 x 4

Return Telephone Call: Japan Trip

You will participate in a simulated telephone conversation with someone you are calling back after receiving a message. First, you will listen to the voice message. Then the telephone call will begin. Each time it is your turn to speak, you will have 20 seconds to record. You should respond as fully and as appropriately as possible.

(Narrator)   Listen to the voice message.

(Man)

(Narrator)   Now the telephone call will begin. After the phone is answered, begin with a greeting and then explain why you are calling.

(Man)   [Telephone] [Rings twice and picks up]

(20 seconds)

(Man)

(20 seconds)

(Man)

(20 seconds)

(Man)

(20 seconds)

<話す School Announcement アドバイス>

【Knowledge/skills】
- Presentational communication
- Informing

【Format】
- 1 question, 10 points, 1 minute to prepare & 1 minute to record

【Speech style】
For public speaking, use the polite です/ます style.

【Structure】
1. Opening remark:
   こんにちは、皆さん。これから、(topic) についてのお知らせをします。
2. Information
3. Closing remark:
   では、どうぞよろしくお願いいたします。以上です。

【Helpful word list】
1. Welcome, everyone. →ようこそ、皆さん。
2. ～月 (ex. 4月、9月)
3. ～日 (ex. 1日、１０日, etc.)
4. ～曜日
5. 午前、午後、～時、～分
6. 4:00 p.m. on Saturday, March 10th →三月十日土曜日の午後４時
7. Place で Event があります。
   There is a basketball game at the gym. 体育館でバスケットの試合があります。
8. Meeting time →集合時間〔しゅうごうじかん〕or 集まる時間
9. Meeting place →集合場所〔しゅうごうばしょ〕or 集まる場所
10. Departure time →出発時間〔しゅっぱつじかん〕
11. Arrival time →到着時間〔とうちゃくじかん〕
12. Be on time. →時間を守って下さい。

話：お知らせ

13. Things you may bring are 〜. →持って来てもいい物は〜です。
14. Things you may not bring are 〜. →持って来てはいけない物は〜です。
15. RSVP →出席〔しゅっせき〕か欠席〔けっせき〕を知らせて下さい。
16. Please contact. →連絡〔れんらく〕してください。
17. by April 15 →４月１５日までに
18. deadline →締め切り〔しめきり〕
19. valuables →貴重品〔きちょうひん〕
20. Please turn in. →提出〔ていしゅつ〕して下さい。or 出して下さい。
21. That's all. →以上〔いじょう〕です。

【Suggestion】
Speak clearly, loudly, cheerfully, pleasantly and politely.

＜１・話す（学校アナウンス）＞

10点
1分＋1分

School Announcement: Welcome Reception

Directions: Imagine that you are making a podcast announcement in Japanese to advertise the school carnival to Japanese-speaking people at your school. First, you will see some notes in English about what to include in your announcement. You will have 1 minute to prepare your announcement while you look at the notes. Then you will have 1 minute to record your announcement. Your announcement should have an opening remark, details based on the notes, and a closing remark. Deliver your announcement using complete sentences in *desu/masu* style.

Japanese Club Welcome Reception
Saturday, September 20, 4:30 p.m. - 7:00 p.m.
Location: school cafeteria
Things to bring: favorite dish, drink
RSVP to Japanese Club by Friday, September 19, 3:00 p.m.

＜２・話す（学校アナウンス）＞

10点
1分＋1分

School Announcement: Musical Performance

Directions: Imagine that you are making a podcast announcement in Japanese to advertise a school musical performance to Japanese-speaking people. First, you will see some notes in English about what to include in your announcement.   You will have 1 minute to prepare your announcement while you look at the notes. Then you will have 1 minute to record your announcement. Your announcement should have an opening remark, details based on the notes, and a closing remark. Deliver your announcement using complete sentences in *desu/masu* style.

Musical "Mikado" performance
Friday, April 24, 6:30 p.m. - 8:00 p.m.
Kennedy High School auditorium
All reserved seats
$10 admission fee
Tickets on sale at the box office from tomorrow between 12:00 - 4:30

話：お知らせ

＜３・話す（学校アナウンス）＞

10点
1分+1分

School Announcement: School Visit

Directions: Imagine that you are making a podcast announcement in Japanese to Japanese-speaking students visiting your school. First, you will see some notes in English about what to include in your announcement. You will have 1 minute to prepare your announcement while you look at the notes. Then you will have 1 minute to record your announcement. Your announcement should have an opening remark, details based on the notes, and a closing remark. Deliver your announcement using complete sentences in *desu/masu* style.

Visit your assigned student's classes.
Follow today's schedule. Today is Tuesday, October 10.
Two American students are assigned to host one Japanese student.
The list shows who your partners are.
Eat lunch at 11:30 - 12:30 with both American students.
Pay for your own lunch.
Return to this same place by 3:00 pm.

＜４・話す（学校アナウンス）＞

10点
1分＋1分

School Announcement: Community Service

Directions: Imagine that you are making a podcast announcement in Japanese to inform Japanese about a beach clean-up. First, you will see some notes in English about what students to include in your announcement. You will have 1 minute to prepare your announcement while you look at the notes. Then you will have 1 minute to record your announcement. Your announcement should have an opening remark, details based on the notes, and a closing remark. Deliver your announcement using complete sentences in *desu/masu* style.

Community service - Beach clean-up.
Sunday, March 10, 8:30 a.m. - 12:00
Meet in front of the school gate at 7:45 a.m.
The school bus will leave at 8:00 a.m.
Bring trash bags, gloves, tools to pick up trash.
Attire - shorts, T-shirt, comfortable footwear, cap, sunscreen
Free lunch and drinks will be provided.

＜５・話す（学校アナウンス）＞

10点
1分＋1分

School Announcement: Dress Code

Directions: Imagine that you are making a podcast announcement in Japanese to inform Japanese students about your school's attire policy. First, you will see some notes in English about what to include in your announcement. You will have 1 minute to prepare your announcement while you look at the notes. Then you will have 1 minute to record your announcement. Your announcement should have an opening remark, details based on the notes, and a closing remark. Deliver your announcement using complete sentences in *desu/masu* style.

School attire policy:
Shirts with the school logo, long pants for boys, skirts for girls
All shirts must be long enough so that the midriff is not exposed.
No portion of a student's underwear may be visible.
This policy is in effect on campus on school days between 7:30 a.m. - 3:30 p.m.
Offenders will receive demerits.

＜6・話す（学校アナウンス）＞

10点
1分＋1分

School Announcement: School Cellular Phone Rules

Directions: Imagine that you are making a podcast announcement in Japanese to inform Japanese visitors about your school's cellular phone policy. First, you will see some notes in English about what to include in your announcement. You will have 1 minute to prepare your announcement while you look at the notes. Then you will have 1 minute to record your announcement. Your announcement should have an opening remark, details based on the notes, and a closing remark. Deliver your announcement using complete sentences in *desu/masu* style.

School cellular phone rules effective from September 1st.
Turn off all cellular phones in the classrooms.
Cellular phone use not allowed in the classrooms.
If your cellular phone rings in class, teachers may confiscate it from you.
If your cellular phone is confiscated by a teacher, you must report to the principal's office by 3:30 p.m. of the same day.

話：お知らせ

＜7・話す（学校アナウンス）＞

10点
1分＋1分

School Announcement: Computer Laboratory

Directions: Imagine that you are making a podcast announcement in Japanese to inform Japanese visitors about your school's computer lab. First, you will see some notes in English about what to include in your announcement. You will have 1 minute to prepare your announcement while you look at the notes. Then you will have 1 minute to record your announcement. Your announcement should have an opening remark, details based on the notes, and a closing remark. Deliver your announcement using complete sentences in *desu/masu* style.

Computer lab:
Located on the ground floor of the school library.
Open daily between 7:30 a.m. - 4:00 p.m.
Need a school I.D. and password.
No drink, no food, no computer games.
Closed on the second and fourth Friday afternoons.
2 technology staff assistants are available.

<8・話す（学校アナウンス）>

10点
1分+1分

School Announcement: College Fair

Directions: Imagine that you are making a podcast announcement in Japanese to inform Japanese visitors about a college fair at your school. First, you will see some notes in English about what to include in your announcement. You will have 1 minute to prepare your announcement while you look at the notes. Then you will have 1 minute to record your announcement. Your announcement should have an opening remark, details based on the notes, and a closing remark. Deliver your announcement using complete sentences in *desu/masu* style.

College Fair:
Date: Friday, November 27th
Time: 3:00 p.m. - 6:30 p.m.
Place: In the cafeteria
Presenters: Alumni from 40 different universities
Refreshment and light snacks provided.
Admission: Free

話：お知らせ

<9・話す（学校アナウンス）>

10点
1分＋1分

School Announcement: Carnival

Directions: Imagine that you are making a podcast announcement in Japanese to advertise the school carnival to Japanese-speaking visitors. First, you will see some notes in English about what to include in your announcement. You will have 1 minute to prepare your announcement while you look at the notes. Then you will have 1 minute to record your announcement. Your announcement should have an opening remark, details based on the notes, and a closing remark. Deliver your announcement using complete sentences in *desu/masu* style.

Carnival:
Friday, Feb. 2nd, 11:00 a.m. - 11:00 p.m. and Saturday Feb. 3rd, 11:00 a.m. - 11:00 p.m.
On the school grounds.
Theme: Pacific and Asia
Variety of ethnic food, drinks, games, rides, art, plants, fruits and vegetables, etc.
Volunteers: parents, students, teachers, alumni, etc.
Purpose: to raise money for scholarships and school facilities.
Goal: $1,000,000
Admission: Free

話：お知らせ

<10・話す（学校アナウンス）>

10点
1分＋1分

School Announcement: Typhoon Warning

Directions: Imagine that you are making a podcast announcement in Japanese to inform Japanese visitors on your campus about an impending typhoon. First, you will see some notes in English about what to include in your announcement. You will have 1 minute to prepare your announcement while you look at the notes. Then you will have 1 minute to record your announcement. Your announcement should have an opening remark, details based on the notes, and a closing remark. Deliver your announcement using complete sentences in *desu/masu* style.

Emergency typhoon warning:
Typhoon is approaching our area.
School will be closed at 11:30 a.m. today.
Return home quickly and safely.
Be careful of heavy rain and strong winds.
Listen to the radio for tomorrow's school schedule.

<11・話す（学校アナウンス）>

10点
1分＋1分

School Announcement: Bento Sale

Directions: Imagine that you are making a podcast announcement in Japanese to advertise an *bento* sale fundraiser to some Japanese visitors. First, you will see some notes in English about what to include in your announcement. You will have 1 minute to prepare your announcement while you look at the notes. Then you will have 1 minute to record your announcement. Your announcement should have an opening remark, details based on the notes, and a closing remark. Deliver your announcement using complete sentences in *desu/masu* style.

Bento sale:
Fund raising for Japan Club
Monday, May 5th
9:30 a.m. until bento sells out.
Bento price is $5.50. Drinks are $1.00.
Bento includes rice, garlic fried chicken, hot dog, pickled *daikon*

話：お知らせ

<12・話す（学校アナウンス）>

10点
1分+1分

School Announcement: Mother's Day Bazaar

Directions: Imagine that you are making a podcast announcement in Japanese to advertise a Mother's Day Bazaar at your school to Japanese-speaking visitors. First, you will see some notes in English about what to include in your announcement. You will have 1 minute to prepare your announcement while you look at the notes. Then you will have 1 minute to record your announcement. Your announcement should have an opening remark, details based on the notes, and a closing remark. Deliver your announcement using complete sentences in *desu/masu* style.

Mother's Day Bazaar:
Thursday and Friday, May 8th and 9th
7:30 a.m. - 3:00 p.m.
School parking lot under the tent
Jewelry, bags, gift items, clothing, baked goods and lots more
Fresh flowers from Rainbow Florist: Roses, spring bouquets, tulips and more!

話：お知らせ

<13・話す（学校アナウンス）>

10点
1分+1分

School Announcement: Speech Contest

Directions: Imagine that you are making a podcast announcement in Japanese to inform Japanese-speaking visitors about a speech contest for students of Japanese. First, you will see some notes in English about what to include in your announcement. You will have 1 minute to prepare your announcement while you look at the notes. Then you will have 1 minute to record your announcement. Your announcement should have an opening remark, details based on the notes, and a closing remark. Deliver your announcement using complete sentences in *desu/masu* style.

Japanese language speech contest for high school students.
Saturday, April 4th, 9:00 a.m. - 12:00
Tokai University Auditorium (7th floor)
About 30 participants from both private and public high schools from throughout the state.
Prizes: 1 night stay at the Sheraton Hotel, gift certificates to restaurants, etc.
One top winner to the national speech tournament in L.A.
For more information, call 823-5701.

＜話す Story Narration アドバイス＞

【Knowledge/skills】
- Presentational communication
- Narrating a story as depicted by a series of pictures

【Format】
- 1 question, 10 points, 4 minutes to prepare and 2 minutes to record

【Speech style】
For story narrations, use the polite です/ます style.

【Helpful Sentence Structures】
1. Command forms
   a. Command form
      お父さんが「早く決めろ。」と言いました。Father said, "Decide soon."
   b. Negative command form
      お父さんが「走るな。」と言いました。Father said, "Don't run."
   c. Polite command form
      お母さんが「早く決めなさい。」と言いました。Mother said, "Decide soon."
   d. Negative polite command form
      お母さんが「走らないで or 走ってはだめ。」と言いました。
      Mother said, "Don't run."
2. Quotations
   a. Direct quotation
      お母さんが「早く決めなさい。」と言いました。Mother said "Decide soon."
   b. Indirect quotation
      お母さんが早く決めるように言いました。Mother said to decide soon.
   c. Question word in direct quotation
      何を食べようかと考えています。He is thinking about what to eat.
3. Complex sentences
   a. 音楽を聞きながら、お皿を洗っています。
      She is washing dishes while listening to music.
   b. 食べた後、買い物に行きました。After eating, she went shopping.
   c. 起きて、シャワーをあびています。He woke up and is taking a shower.

話：漫画

d. 寝る前に、歯をみがいています。She is brushing her teeth before she goes to bed.
e. 寝る時に、本を読みます。Before she goes to bed, she reads a book.
f. お母さんが料理をしている間に、お父さんは掃除をしています。
   While mother is cooking, father is cleaning.
g. 夕食を食べてから、宿題をしました。After eating dinner, she did her homework.
h. お母さんは子供がまだ寝ているのを見ました。Mother saw her child still sleeping.
i. 何度じゃんけんしても、決まりません。Even though they did *jankenpo* many times, it was undecided.

4. Conditional
   a. 右にまがると、大きいデパートがあります。
      When you turn right, there is a large department store.
   b. 早く終わったら、買い物に行きましょう。
      If we finish early, let's go shopping.
   c. 雨が降らなければ、ピクニックをします。
      If and only if it does not rain, we will have a picnic.

5. Stative conditions
   a. ドアが開いています。The door is open.
   b. ドアが閉まっています。The door is closed.
   c. テレビがついています。The TV is on.
   d. テレビが消えています。The TV is off.
   e. 絵がかべにかけてあります。A painting has been hung on the wall.
   f. お花がかざってあります。Flowers have been decorated.

6. Compare:
   a. 電気がついています。The lights are on.
   b. 電気がつけてあります。The lights have been turned on.
   c. 電気をつけています。(Someone) is turning on the lights.

【Suggestions】
1. Narrate a story; do not write a skit.
2. Be creative, but make sure your story follows the pictures given.
3. Use past tense.
4. Express yourself dramatically.
5. Speak clearly and loudly.
6. Use a confident tone of voice.

＜１・話す（四コマ漫画）＞

Story Narration: Morning Rush

10点
4分+2分

Directions: Imagine that you are making an oral presentation to your Japanese class. In your presentation, you will narrate a story. First, you will see pictures depicting the story. You will have 4 minutes to prepare your narration while you look at the pictures. Then you will have 2 minutes to record your narration. Narrate your story using complete sentences in *desu/masu* style.

＜２・話す（四コマ漫画）＞

Story Narration: Karaoke

10点
4分+2分

Directions: Imagine that you are making an oral presentation to your Japanese class. In your presentation, you will narrate a story. First, you will see pictures depicting the story. You will have 4 minutes to prepare your narration while you look at the pictures. Then you will have 2 minutes to record your narration. Narrate your story using complete sentences in *desu/masu* style.

話：漫画

＜３・話す（四コマ漫画）＞

10点
4分+2分

Story Narration: Recycling

Directions: Imagine that you are making an oral presentation to your Japanese class. In your presentation, you will narrate a story. First, you will see pictures depicting the story. You will have 4 minutes to prepare your narration while you look at the pictures. Then you will have 2 minutes to record your narration. Narrate your story using complete sentences in *desu/masu* style.

話：漫画

＜4・話す（四コマ漫画）＞

10点
4分＋2分

Story Narration: Observing Obon

Directions: Imagine that you are making an oral presentation to your Japanese class. In your presentation, you will narrate a story. First, you will see pictures depicting the story. You will have 4 minutes to prepare your narration while you look at the pictures. Then you will have 2 minutes to record your narration. Narrate your story using complete sentences in *desu/masu* style.

話：漫画

＜5・話す（四コマ漫画）＞

10点
4分+2分

Story Narration: Graduation

Directions: Imagine that you are making an oral presentation to your Japanese class. In your presentation, you will narrate a story. First, you will see pictures depicting the story. You will have 4 minutes to prepare your narration while you look at the pictures. Then you will have 2 minutes to record your narration. Narrate your story using complete sentences in *desu/masu* style.

話：漫画

＜6・話す（四コマ漫画）＞

10点
4分+2分

Story Narration: Cellular Phones

Directions: Imagine that you are making an oral presentation to your Japanese class. In your presentation, you will narrate a story. First, you will see pictures depicting the story. You will have 4 minutes to prepare your narration while you look at the pictures. Then you will have 2 minutes to record your narration. Narrate your story using complete sentences in *desu/masu* style.

話：漫画

＜７・話す（四コマ漫画）＞

10点
4分+2分

Story Narration: Robots

Directions: Imagine that you are making an oral presentation to your Japanese class. In your presentation, you will narrate a story. First, you will see pictures depicting the story. You will have 4 minutes to prepare your narration while you look at the pictures. Then you will have 2 minutes to record your narration. Narrate your story using complete sentences in *desu/masu* style.

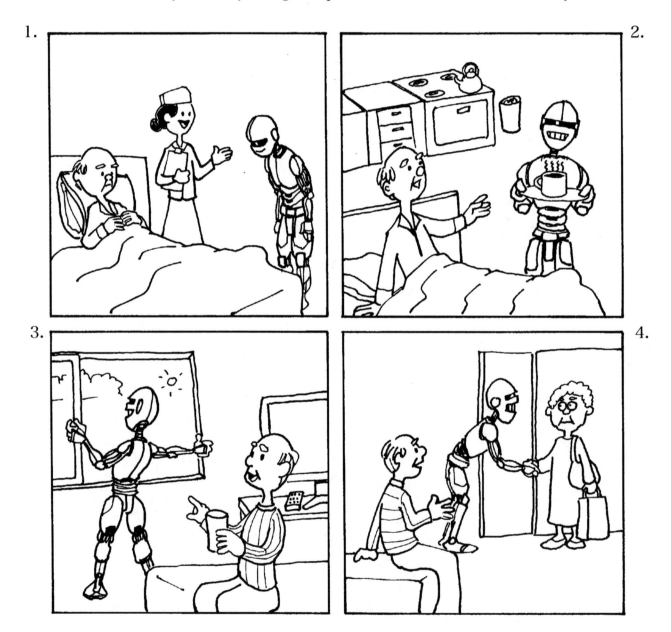

話：漫画

＜8・話す（四コマ漫画）＞

10点
4分+2分

Story Narration: Part-time Job

Directions: Imagine that you are making an oral presentation to your Japanese class. In your presentation, you will narrate a story. First, you will see pictures depicting the story. You will have 4 minutes to prepare your narration while you look at the pictures. Then you will have 2 minutes to record your narration. Narrate your story using complete sentences in *desu/masu* style.

話：漫画

<9・話す（四コマ漫画）>

10点
4分+2分

Story Narration: New Year's Day

Directions: Imagine that you are making an oral presentation to your Japanese class. In your presentation, you will narrate a story. First, you will see pictures depicting the story. You will have 4 minutes to prepare your narration while you look at the pictures. Then you will have 2 minutes to record your narration. Narrate your story using complete sentences in *desu/masu* style.

話：漫画

<10・話す（四コマ漫画）>

10点
4分+2分

Story Narration: Traffic Accident

Directions: Imagine that you are making an oral presentation to your Japanese class. In your presentation, you will narrate a story. First, you will see pictures depicting the story. You will have 4 minutes to prepare your narration while you look at the pictures. Then you will have 2 minutes to record your narration. Narrate your story using complete sentences in *desu/masu* style.

話：漫画

<11・話す（四コマ漫画）>

Story Narration: Shopping

10点
4分+2分

Directions: Imagine that you are making an oral presentation to your Japanese class. In your presentation, you will narrate a story. First, you will see pictures depicting the story. You will have 4 minutes to prepare your narration while you look at the pictures. Then you will have 2 minutes to record your narration. Narrate your story using complete sentences in *desu/masu* style.

1.

2.

3.

4.

話：漫画

<12・話す（四コマ漫画）>

10点
4分+2分

Story Narration: Illness

Directions: Imagine that you are making an oral presentation to your Japanese class. In your presentation, you will narrate a story. First, you will see pictures depicting the story. You will have 4 minutes to prepare your narration while you look at the pictures. Then you will have 2 minutes to record your narration. Narrate your story using complete sentences in *desu/masu* style.

話：漫画

<13・話す（四コマ漫画）>

10点
4分＋2分

Story Narration: Internationalization

Directions: Imagine that you are making an oral presentation to your Japanese class. In your presentation, you will narrate a story. First, you will see pictures depicting the story. You will have 4 minutes to prepare your narration while you look at the pictures. Then you will have 2 minutes to record your narration. Narrate your story using complete sentences in *desu/masu* style.

話：漫画

<話す Cultural Perspective Presentation アドバイス>

【Knowledge/skills】
- Presentational communication (speaking)
- Describing and expressing your opinion about a Japanese cultural practice or product

【Format】
- 1 question, 10 points, 4 minutes to prepare and 2 minutes to record

【Speech style】
Use polite です/ます style.

【Sample structure】
1. Begin with an appropriate introduction.
   これから、(topic) について話します。
2. Discuss five aspects of the topic.
   1.) まず or 第一に、
   2.) 次に or 第二に、
   3.) 第三に、
   4.) 第四に、
   5.) 第五に、
3. Explain your view or perspective.
   私の考えとして、〜と思います。
4. End with a concluding remark.
   最後に、〜。 以上です。

【Helpful words】
1. Conjunction words
   a. それから、：Then,
   b. そのうえ、：Besides, moreover
   c. しかも、：Besides, moreover
   d. それとも、：Or
   e. ですから、：Therefore,
   f. しかし、：However,
   g. 一般的〔いっぱんてき〕に言って、：Generally speaking,

  h. たとえば：For instance,
  i. なぜなら、〜からです。：That's because 〜
2. Uncertainty
  a. 日本人は魚をよく食べる<u>ようです</u>。Japanese seem to eat a lot of fish.
  b. 日本人は魚をよく食べる<u>らしいです</u>。Japanese seem to eat a lot of fish.
  c. 日本人は魚をよく食べる<u>かもしれない</u>。Japanese might eat a lot of fish.
  d. 日本人は魚をよく食べる<u>にちがいありません</u>。Japanese must eat a lot of fish.
  e. 日本人は魚をよく食べ<u>そうです</u>。It seems Japanese eat a lot of fish.
  f. 日本人は魚をよく食べる<u>そうです</u>。I heard that Japanese eat a lot of fish.

【Suggestions】
1. Make sure to speak loudly and clearly. Use a confident voice.
2. Learn about Japanese culture with accuracy and details.
3. Observe and think critically about reasons for Japanese cultural behavior.
4. If you are not sure about aspects of Japanese culture you are discussing, use grammar forms that express uncertainty.

< 1・話す（文化）>

10点
4分+2分

Cultural Perspective Presentation: Japanese Greetings

Directions: Imagine you are making an oral presentation to your Japanese class. First, you will read and hear the topic for your presentation. You will have 4 minutes to prepare your presentation. Then you will have 2 minutes to record your presentation. Your presentation should be as complete as possible.

Present your own view or perspective of Japanese greetings. Discuss at least FIVE aspects or examples of Japanese greetings.

Begin with an appropriate introduction, give details, explain your own view or perspective, and end with a concluding remark.

【Let's take notes!】

1. Begin with an appropriate introduction.

   _____

2. Discuss five aspects/examples of the topic.

   1.) _____
   2.) _____
   3.) _____
   4.) _____
   5.) _____

3. Explain your view or perspective.

   _____

4. End with a concluding remark.

   _____

話：文化

＜２・話す（文化）＞

10点
4分＋2分

Cultural Perspective Presentation: Japanese Pop Culture

Directions: Imagine you are making an oral presentation to your Japanese class. First, you will read and hear the topic for your presentation. You will have 4 minutes to prepare your presentation. Then you will have 2 minutes to record your presentation. Your presentation should be as complete as possible.

Present your own view or perspective of Japanese pop culture. Discuss at least FIVE aspects or examples of Japanese pop culture.

Begin with an appropriate introduction, give details, explain your own view or perspective, and end with a concluding remark.

【Let's take notes!】

1. Begin with an appropriate introduction.
   _____

2. Discuss five aspects/examples of the topic.
   1.) _____
   2.) _____
   3.) _____
   4.) _____
   5.) _____

3. Explain your view or perspective.
   _____

4. End with a concluding remark.
   _____

<3・話す（文化）>

10点
4分+2分

Cultural Perspective Presentation: Japanese Houses

Directions: Imagine you are making an oral presentation to your Japanese class. First, you will read and hear the topic for your presentation. You will have 4 minutes to prepare your presentation. Then you will have 2 minutes to record your presentation. Your presentation should be as complete as possible.

Present your own view or perspective of Japanese houses. Discuss at least FIVE aspects or examples of Japanese houses.

Begin with an appropriate introduction, give details, explain your own view or perspective, and end with a concluding remark.

【Let's take notes!】

1. Begin with an appropriate introduction.

   _____

2. Discuss five aspects/examples of the topic.

   1.) _____
   2.) _____
   3.) _____
   4.) _____
   5.) _____

3. Explain your view or perspective.

   _____

4. End with a concluding remark.

   _____

＜４・話す（文化）＞

10点
4分+2分

Cultural Perspective Presentation: Geography of Japan

Directions: Imagine you are making an oral presentation to your Japanese class. First, you will read and hear the topic for your presentation. You will have 4 minutes to prepare your presentation. Then you will have 2 minutes to record your presentation. Your presentation should be as complete as possible.

Present your own view or perspective of the geography of Japan. Discuss at least FIVE aspects or examples of Japanese geography.

Begin with an appropriate introduction, give details, explain your own view or perspective, and end with a concluding remark.

【Let's take notes!】

1. Begin with an appropriate introduction.
   _____

2. Discuss five aspects/examples of the topic.
   1.) _____
   2.) _____
   3.) _____
   4.) _____
   5.) _____

3. Explain your view or perspective.
   _____

4. End with a concluding remark.
   _____

＜５・話す（文化）＞

10点
4分+2分

Cultural Perspective Presentation: Japanese Fashion

Directions: Imagine you are making an oral presentation to your Japanese class. First, you will read and hear the topic for your presentation. You will have 4 minutes to prepare your presentation. Then you will have 2 minutes to record your presentation. Your presentation should be as complete as possible.

Present your own view or perspective of Japanese fashion. Discuss at least FIVE aspects or examples of Japanese fashion.

Begin with an appropriate introduction, give details, explain your own view or perspective, and end with a concluding remark.

【Let's take notes!】

1. Begin with an appropriate introduction.

   _____

2. Discuss five aspects/examples of the topic.

   1.) _____
   2.) _____
   3.) _____
   4.) _____
   5.) _____

3. Explain your view or perspective.

   _____

4. End with a concluding remark.

   _____

話：文化

＜6・話す（文化）＞

10点
4分+2分

Cultural Perspective Presentation: Japanese Entertainment

Directions: Imagine you are making an oral presentation to your Japanese class. First, you will read and hear the topic for your presentation. You will have 4 minutes to prepare your presentation. Then you will have 2 minutes to record your presentation. Your presentation should be as complete as possible.

Present your own view or perspective of Japanese entertainment. Discuss at least FIVE aspects or examples of Japanese entertainment.

Begin with an appropriate introduction, give details, explain your own view or perspective, and end with a concluding remark.

【Let's take notes!】

1. Begin with an appropriate introduction.
   _____

2. Discuss five aspects/examples of the topic.
   1.) _____
   2.) _____
   3.) _____
   4.) _____
   5.) _____

3. Explain your view or perspective.
   _____

4. End with a concluding remark.
   _____

話：文化

＜７・話す（文化）＞

10点
4分+2分

Cultural Perspective Presentation: Japanese Technology

Directions: Imagine you are making an oral presentation to your Japanese class. First, you will read and hear the topic for your presentation. You will have 4 minutes to prepare your presentation. Then you will have 2 minutes to record your presentation. Your presentation should be as complete as possible.

Present your own view or perspective of Japanese technology. Discuss at least FIVE aspects or examples of Japanese technology.

Begin with an appropriate introduction, give details, explain your own view or perspective, and end with a concluding remark.

【Let's take notes!】

1. Begin with an appropriate introduction.
   _____

2. Discuss five aspects/examples of the topic.
   1.) _____
   2.) _____
   3.) _____
   4.) _____
   5.) _____

3. Explain your view or perspective.
   _____

4. End with a concluding remark.
   _____

話：文化

＜8・話す（文化）＞

10点
4分+2分

Cultural Perspective Presentation: Japanese Work Etiquette

Directions: Imagine you are making an oral presentation to your Japanese class. First, you will read and hear the topic for your presentation. You will have 4 minutes to prepare your presentation. Then you will have 2 minutes to record your presentation. Your presentation should be as complete as possible.

Present your own view or perspective of Japanese work etiquette. Discuss at least FIVE aspects or examples of Japanese manners at work.

Begin with an appropriate introduction, give details, explain your own view or perspective, and end with a concluding remark.

【Let's take notes!】

1. Begin with an appropriate introduction.
   _____

2. Discuss five aspects/examples of the topic.

   1.) _____
   2.) _____
   3.) _____
   4.) _____
   5.) _____

3. Explain your view or perspective.
   _____

4. End with a concluding remark.
   _____

話：文化

＜9・話す（文化）＞

10点　4分＋2分

Cultural Perspective Presentation: Japanese Traditional Culture

Directions: Imagine you are making an oral presentation to your Japanese class. First, you will read and hear the topic for your presentation. You will have 4 minutes to prepare your presentation. Then you will have 2 minutes to record your presentation. Your presentation should be as full as possible.

Present your own view or perspective of Japanese traditional culture. Discuss at least FIVE aspects or examples of Japanese traditional culture.

Begin with an appropriate introduction, give details, explain your own view or perspective, and end with a concluding remark.

【Let's take notes!】

1. Begin with an appropriate introduction.
   _____

2. Discuss five aspects/examples of the topic.
   1.) _____
   2.) _____
   3.) _____
   4.) _____
   5.) _____

3. Explain your view or perspective.
   _____

4. End with a concluding remark.
   _____

<10・話す（文化）>

10点
4分+2分

Cultural Perspective Presentation: Japanese Climate

Directions: Imagine you are making an oral presentation to your Japanese class. First, you will read and hear the topic for your presentation. You will have 4 minutes to prepare your presentation. Then you will have 2 minutes to record your presentation. Your presentation should be as complete as possible.

Present your own view or perspective of the Japanese climate. Discuss at least FIVE aspects or examples of the climate of Japan.

Begin with an appropriate introduction, give details, explain your own view or perspective, and end with a concluding remark.

【Let's take notes!】

1. Begin with an appropriate introduction.
   _____

2. Discuss five aspects/examples of the topic.
   1.) _____
   2.) _____
   3.) _____
   4.) _____
   5.) _____

3. Explain your view or perspective.
   _____

4. End with a concluding remark.
   _____

<11・話す（文化）>

**10点
4分+2分**

Cultural Perspective Presentation: Japanese Cooking

Directions: Imagine you are making an oral presentation to your Japanese class. First, you will read and hear the topic for your presentation. You will have 4 minutes to prepare your presentation. Then you will have 2 minutes to record your presentation. Your presentation should be as complete as possible.

Present your own view or perspective of Japanese cooking. Discuss at least FIVE aspects or examples of Japanese cooking.

Begin with an appropriate introduction, give details, explain your own view or perspective, and end with a concluding remark.

【Let's take notes!】

1. Begin with an appropriate introduction.
   _____

2. Discuss five aspects/examples of the topic.
   1.) _____
   2.) _____
   3.) _____
   4.) _____
   5.) _____

3. Explain your view or perspective.
   _____

4. End with a concluding remark.
   _____

話：文化

<12・話す（文化）>

10点
4分+2分

Cultural Perspective Presentation: Japanese Currency

Directions: Imagine you are making an oral presentation to your Japanese class. First, you will read and hear the topic for your presentation. You will have 4 minutes to prepare your presentation. Then you will have 2 minutes to record your presentation. Your presentation should be as complete as possible.

Present your own view or perspective of Japanese currency. Discuss at least FIVE aspects or examples of Japanese currency.

Begin with an appropriate introduction, give details, explain your own view or perspective, and end with a concluding remark.

【Let's take notes!】

1. Begin with an appropriate introduction.

   _____

2. Discuss five aspects/examples of the topic.

   1.) _____

   2.) _____

   3.) _____

   4.) _____

   5.) _____

3. Explain your view or perspective.

   _____

4. End with a concluding remark.

   _____

話：文化

<13・話す（文化）>

10点
4分+2分

Cultural Perspective Presentation: Japanese International Problems

Directions: Imagine you are making an oral presentation to your Japanese class. First, you will read and hear the topic for your presentation. You will have 4 minutes to prepare your presentation. Then you will have 2 minutes to record your presentation. Your presentation should be as complete as possible.

Present your own view or perspective of Japanese international problems. Discuss at least FIVE aspects or examples of Japanese international problems.

Begin with an appropriate introduction, give details, explain your own view or perspective, and end with a concluding remark.

【Let's take notes!】

1. Begin with an appropriate introduction.

   _____

2. Discuss five aspects/examples of the topic.

   1.) _____
   2.) _____
   3.) _____
   4.) _____
   5.) _____

3. Explain your view or perspective.

   _____

4. End with a concluding remark.

   _____

聴解問題と読解問題の答とスクリプト
Answer Key: Listening and Reading Multiple-Choice

This section of the book provides the following, so that you can check your own work and identify any areas that need more practice. To evaluate your answers to the free-response (writing and speaking) questions, you can also refer to the scoring guidelines available from the College Board at http://www.collegeboard.com/student/testing/ap/japanese/samp.html?japaneselag.

1. 聴解問題のスクリプトと答	Listening Scripts & Answers	p. 181
2. 読解問題の答	Reading Answers	p. 207
3. 会話問題のスクリプト	Conversation Scripts	p. 222
4. 留守番電話問題のスクリプト	Return Telephone Call Scripts	p. 235

<1・聞く>

Listening: Home Delivery

(Narrator)　Now you will listen once to a prerecorded message.

(Clerk)　荷物はひとつでございますか。スーツケースだけでよろしいですね。スーツケースの中にこわれ物とかございませんか。すみませんが、こちらの送り状にご記入ください。太線枠内をボールペンで強くご記入ください。まず、こちらにお届け先の郵便番号と電話番号とご住所と氏名をご記入ください。お届け先は、郵便番号６０３－８２０４、京都市北区紫竹高縄町（しちくたかなわ）２０－５近藤利彦（こんどうとしひこ）様方ケン・スミス様でございますね。そして、こちらに御依頼主（ごいらいぬし）様のお名前をご記入ください。ご希望のお届け日がある場合は、こちらに何月何日とご記入ください。４月２日でよろしいですね。またご希望のお届け時間帯がございましたら、こちらに丸をしてください。午前中か１２時から１４時の間、１４時から１６時の間、１６時から１８時の間、１８時から２０時の間、２０時から２１時の間のおひとつをお選びください。１４時から１６時の間でよろしいですね。では、料金は１，７９０円になります。では、お荷物は明日（あした）こちらのご住所にお届けいたします。ありがとうございました。

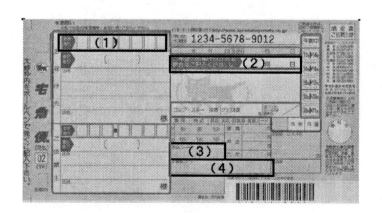

< 1 ・聞く (質問) >   * Correct answer

Listening: Home Delivery

(Narrator)   Now answer the questions for this selection.

1. How many pieces of luggage did Ken take to the *Takkyuubin* counter?
    (A)   Ken took one suitcase. *
    (B)   Ken took one suitcase and another fragile box.
    (C)   Ken took two suitcases.
    (D)   Ken took one fragile box.

2. What directions did Ken hear from the clerk?
    (A)   To complete the form in pencil.
    (B)   To complete the form with a red ballpoint pen.
    (C)   To complete only the section inside the bold lines. *
    (D)   To complete only the underlined parts of the form.

3. What did Ken have to write on the form?
    (A)   Receiver's address and full name.
    (B)   Receiver's address, full name and telephone number.
    (C)   Sender's address, zip code, full name and telephone number.
    (D)   Receiver's address, zip code, full name and telephone number. *

4. What address is Ken sending his luggage to?
    (A)   A location where the zip code is 603-8024.
    (B)   The west district of Kyoto.
    (C)   The south district of Kyoto.
    (D)   The receiver is Ken himself, but Ken sent it to Mr. Kondo's address. *

5. When does Ken want the luggage delivered?
    (A)   Ken wants it delivered between 2:00 and 4:00 p.m. on 4/1.
    (B)   Ken wants it delivered between 2:00 and 4:00 p.m. on 4/2. *
    (C)   Ken wants it delivered between 4:00 and 6:00 p.m. on 4/1.
    (D)   Ken wants it delivered between 4:00 and 6:00 p.m. on 4/2.

<２・聞く>

Listening: Internationalization of Sports

(Narrator)　Now you will listen once to a conversation.

(Man)　最近、相撲取りに外国人が多いね。今場所、１４勝１敗で優勝したのもモンゴル出身の人だったし、ロシア人や東ヨーロッパの相撲取りもいたね。でも、ハワイからの相撲取りを見なかったね。青い目の金髪の相撲取りが、ちょんまげを結って、まわしをしめて、相撲をしているのは、ちょっと変じゃないかな。でも、皆日本語が上手なのはすごいね。

(Woman)　私はスポーツの国際化は自然だと思うよ。野球でも大リーグで活躍する日本人選手が増えているし、サッカーでも日本チームの監督はほとんど外国人じゃない？外国人が相撲をして何が悪い？

(Man)　でも、外国人の相撲取りは身長も体重も日本人より上だから、今に日本人の相撲取りはいなくなるんじゃないかな。

(Woman)　私、そうは思わないよ。大きい人が必ず勝つとは言えないから。日本人の中にも強い体を持っている相撲取りもいるし、強い精神力を持っている人もいるし、また強い日本の相撲取りが出て来るわよ。でも、今の若い日本の男性で、相撲のきびしい稽古に耐えられる人って、何人いるかなあ。

<2・聞く (質問)>　　＊ Correct answer

Listening: Internationalization of Sports

(Narrator)　Now answer the questions for this selection.

1. What were the results of the recent sumo tournament?
    (A) A sumo wrestler from Eastern Europe won the tournament with 13 wins and 2 losses.
    (B) A sumo wrestler from Mongolia won the tournament with 14 wins and 1 loss. ＊
    (C) A sumo wrestler from Russia won the tournament with 13 wins and 2 losses.
    (D) A sumo wrestler from Hawaii won the tournament with 14 wins and 1 loss.

2. Where are the recent foreign sumo wrestlers NOT from?
    (A) Mongolia
    (B) Russia
    (C) Eastern Europe
    (D) Hawaii ＊

3. What characteristic of foreign sumo wrestlers impressed the man?
    (A) Their blue eyes
    (B) Their blond hair
    (C) Their hairstyle
    (D) Their Japanese language proficiency ＊

4. What opinion does the woman have about the internationalization of sports?
    (A) She supports the internationalization of sports. ＊
    (B) Japanese baseball players should not play in the American major leagues.
    (C) Japanese soccer teams should not hire foreign managers.
    (D) All sumo wrestlers should be Japanese.

5. What opinion does the woman have about the future of sumo?
    (A) There will be no Japanese wrestlers in the future.
    (B) Foreign sumo wrestlers will be excluded.
    (C) Sumo will become an Olympic sport.
    (D) Not many young Japanese can endure the vigorous sumo practice. ＊

<3・聞く>
Listening: Speech

(Narrator)   Now you will listen once to a speech.

「半分日系半分韓国系」

　僕は半分日系で、半分韓国系です。ですから、僕の人生は大変ですが、おもしろいです。いつも、韓国の文化と日本の文化の間に僕の心の葛藤があります。

　まず、小さい時から日系の家族は、僕に遠慮することを教えました。たとえば、家族でレストランに行って食事をする時に、日本の遠慮の習慣によると、決して最後に残った食べ物を取ってはいけません。しかし、韓国の文化はとても違います。韓国の文化によると、僕は遠慮しないで、その最後に残った食べ物を取るべきです。韓国の文化は、僕に遠慮しないで生きることを教えました。ですから、レストランで家族の食事の終わりになると、僕の心は複雑です。日系マイクは「遠慮しろ！」と言って、韓国マイクは「取れ！」と言っています。そして、僕はいつも困ってしまいます。

　次に、日本文化のほかの大事な事は謙虚です。たとえば、お辞儀の時に、ほかの人よりもっと下に頭を下げるはずです。そして、僕がほめられたら、僕は「いいえ、とんでもないです。」と言わなければなりません。しかし、韓国の文化は違います。韓国の習慣によると、ほめられれば、「有難う」と言ってもかまいません。時々、ほめられて、「有難う」と言わなければ、相手の気持ちを悪くさえするようです。ですから、ほめられた時、僕の心は複雑です。日系マイクは「いいえ、とんでもないですと言え！」と言って、韓国マイクは「有難うと言え！」と言っています。そして、僕はいつも困ってしまいます。

　半分日系で半分韓国系の僕の人生は、ちょっと大変です。日本の文化と韓国の文化は、とても違うので、いつも僕の中で戦っています。しかし、両方の文化が分かるのは、とってもいいことだと思いませんか。

by Michael Lim '07

< 3・聞く(質問) >   * Correct answer

Listening: *Speech*

(Narrator)   Now answer the questions for this selection.

1. What is this person's background?
    (A) He is Korean and is living in Japan.
    (B) He is a Japanese citizen, but his parents are Korean.
    (C) He is ethnically half Korean and half Japanese, and is living in Japan.
    (D) He is half Korean and half Japanese, and is living in the U.S. *

2. What value did he learn from the Japanese side of his family?
    (A) respect
    (B) humility *
    (C) perseverance
    (D) honesty

3. What value did he learn from the Korean side of his family?
    (A) patience
    (B) honor
    (C) trust
    (D) frankness *

4. In what kind of situation does he experience inner conflict?
    (A) When he follows Japanese values.
    (B) When he follows Korean values.
    (C) When he follows his own heart.
    (D) When he is torn about which set of values he should follow. *

5. What is this person's message?
    (A) We should not discriminate based on race.
    (B) We should understand other cultures. *
    (C) We should communicate more with people from other countries.
    (D) We should travel and see other countries.

<4・聞く>

Listening: My Town

(Narrator) Now you will listen once to a presentation.

(Man) 　僕の生まれ育った町、宮島を紹介しましょう。宮島は広島県の瀬戸内海に浮かぶ小さな島です。宮島には平安時代の昔、平清盛という当時の権力者が建てた厳島神社が有名です。潮が満ちると神社は海の中に浮かんでいるようです。水の中に浮かぶ鳥居は、とても美しく有名で、よくポスターになっています。夜ライトアップされて、神秘的です。現在、宮島は世界遺産に指定されていて、訪れる観光客も多いです。夏には花火大会があったり、一年中いろいろなお祭りがあったりして、多くの人達が海外からも訪れます。
　僕の自宅は厳島神社とは少し離れた住宅街にあります。高台なので、坂道を上がったり下りたりしなければなりません。しかし、自宅からは瀬戸内海の美しい海の風景を見渡すことが出来ますし、広島市街地の夜景も見えます。夕焼けや朝日の中に島々が海に浮かぶ風景は、絵のようです。冬には夜空に星がいっぱい見えますし、満月の夜など、こわいくらい美しいです。それに、農業と漁業にたずさわっている人達が多いので、新鮮な野菜や魚を食べることが出来ます。かきは特に有名です。
　しかし、この美しい島も産業と言えば、観光業しかなく、雇用のチャンスが少ないので、若者はだいたい都会へ出て行って、島に帰って来ません。これは島の大きな問題です。旅館やお土産屋を継ぐ若者がなかなかいないそうです。
　僕も都会の大学へ行きたいけど、将来仕事から退職したら、またこの島に戻ってこようと思っています。僕の故郷はこの宮島ですから。

<4・聞く(質問)> * Correct answer

Listening: My Town

(Narrator)   Now answer the questions for this selection.

1. What kind of town does this person live in?
    (A)   His town is a historically famous place. *
    (B)   His town is famous for its natural beauty.
    (C)   His town is famous for an old temple.
    (D)   His town is famous for its unique animals.

2. What kind of place is his town?
    (A)   A famous shrine was built by the water.
    (B)   There is a fireworks show every weekend.
    (C)   There is a famous festival in the fall.
    (D)   Many foreigners visit his town. *

3. What is one good thing about living on this island?
    (A)   People can swim in the ocean.
    (B)   People are kind.
    (C)   People can see lots of stars at night all year long.
    (D)   Vegetables and fish are fresh. *

4. What is a major problem on this person's island?
    (A)   The number of tourists who visit this island is decreasing.
    (B)   Young people who leave do not return to the island. *
    (C)   The fish they can catch around the island is dangerous to eat.
    (D)   The Japanese inns and souvenir shops do not have enough customers.

5. What is this person planning to do in the future?
    (A)   He does not want to leave this island.
    (B)   He wants to return to this island after college.
    (C)   He wants to return to this island after retiring. *
    (D)   He does not want to return to this island at all.

<5・聞く>

Listening: College Entrance

(Narrator)　Now you will listen once to a conversation.

(Man)　日本の大学って、入るのは難しいのに、卒業するのは簡単って聞いたけど、それ、本当？

(Woman)　だいたい当たっているわね。受験勉強が大変すぎるのよ。１月中旬にある一次試験のセンター試験を受けて、その結果はまあまあだったの。その成績で入れそうな国公立大学を一校だけ選ぶことが出来るのよ。大阪大学が希望だったの。３月に大阪大学の二次試験を受験する予定だったのに、その日風邪でものすごい熱、でもがんばって受けたけど、やっぱりすべっちゃった。

(Man)　それは気の毒だったね。試験の一発勝負で決まるなんて、すごいプレッシャーだ。

(Woman)　そうよ。でも、２月に滑り止めの私立大学に合格していたから、気持ちはちょっと楽だった。浪人して予備校へ行くなんて、絶対したくなかったの。

(Man)　アメリカの大学では、だいたいSATの成績と学校での成績で決まるかな。僕は数学や物理が得意だったから、アメリカ西海岸にあるいい工学部がある大学を希望していた。進学の先生と相談したり、コンピューターで調べたりして、６校を選んで、願書を提出したんだ。推薦状も必要だったし、小論文もあったし、一校は面接もあったし、結構大変だったよ。３月末に大学から通知があって、４校に合格してた。その内の一番奨学金をたくさんくれた大学に行くことに決めたんだ。

(Woman)　私もアメリカの入学制度の方がいいと思うな。

<　5・聞く(質問)　>　　　＊ Correct answer

Listening: College Entrance

(Narrator)　Now answer the questions for this selection.

1. What is a correct description of the first exam the woman took?
   (A) The first exam was held in February.
   (B) The results of her first exam were very poor.
   (C) After receiving the results of her first exam, she decided to apply to two national universities.
   (D) After receiving the results of her first exam, she decided to apply to Osaka University. ＊

2. After scheduling a second exam at Osaka University in March, what happened?
   (A) She took the exam and passed it.
   (B) She took the exam, but failed it. ＊
   (C) She didn't take the exam because of a high fever.
   (D) She didn't take the exam because of a traffic accident.

3. What college did this woman go to?
   (A) She was accepted by a national university.
   (B) She was accepted by a private university. ＊
   (C) She decided to reapply to Osaka University the following year.
   (D) She decided to attend a college prep school the following year.

4. What correctly describes this man?
   (A) He was strong in math and physics. ＊
   (B) He wanted to study biology in college.
   (C) He wanted to attend a college on the East Coast.
   (D) He applied to eight universities.

5. What were the results when this man applied to universities in America?
   (A) Recommendations, an essay and an interview were required by all the universities he applied to.
   (B) The results were announced at the beginning of April.
   (C) He was accepted by all the universities he applied to.
   (D) He decided to attend the college that offered the largest scholarship. ＊

＜6・聞く＞

Listening: Cellular Phone Etiquette

(Narrator)　Now you will listen twice to the instructions.

(Woman)　●マナーを守りましょう。
レストラン、ホテルのロビーなどの静かな場所では、静かに話して下さい。「マナーモード」を使うことも出来ます。電車内、バス内で携帯電話で通話することは禁止されています。新幹線や電車などの中では、ほかの人の迷惑にならない場所で携帯電話を使って下さい。歩行中や自転車利用中の携帯電話の使用は、周囲への迷惑になるだけでなく大変危険です。安全な場所に止まるなどしてご利用下さい。
●電源を切りましょう。
劇場や映画館や美術館などでは、電源を切って下さい。飛行機や病院の中は、機械に影響を与える怖れがあるため、電源を切って下さい。電車の優先席付近でも携帯電話の電源を切って下さい。「留守番電話サービス」をご利用になると、電源をオフにしていても、大切なメッセージを逃しません。
●運転中は携帯電話は使わないで下さい。
法律によって、携帯電話を使いながら運転をすると罰金を払わなければなりません。車を止めてから、携帯電話を使って下さい。

(Narrator)　Now listen again.

(Woman)　(Repeat.)

< 6・聞く >   * Correct answer

Listening: Cellular Phone Etiquette

(Narrator)   Now answer the questions for this selection.

1. What cellular phone etiquette is expected in restaurants and hotel lobbies?
   - (A)   No cellular phone use is allowed in either restaurants or hotel lobbies.
   - (B)   Talking quietly on cellular phones is allowed in both restaurants and hotel lobbies. *
   - (C)   Cellphone use is allowed only in restricted areas.
   - (D)   Cellular phone use is allowed in hotel lobbies, but not restaurants.

2. What cellular phone etiquette is expected on public transportation?
   - (A)   People may use cellular phones on the bus.
   - (B)   People may use cellular phones on electric trains.
   - (C)   People may use cellular phones on bullet trains.
   - (D)   People may use cellular phones in a specific restricted area on electric trains and bullet trains. *

3. What will happen to a person who uses a cellular phone while riding a bike in Japan?
   - (A)   It is permissible to use a cellular phone while riding a bicycle.
   - (B)   The cellular phone will be confiscated by the police.
   - (C)   The police will ticket the cellular phone user.
   - (D)   It is illegal, so the person is expected to stop, get off the bike, and use the cellular phone. *

4. In which of the following places is cellular phone use allowed?
   - (A)   Schools. *
   - (B)   Museums and theaters.
   - (C)   Airplanes and hospitals.
   - (D)   Priority seats area on the train.

5. What is the Japanese rule about using a cellular phone while driving?
   - (A)   There is no penalty.
   - (B)   One receives a warning from a police officer.
   - (C)   A fine has to be paid. *
   - (D)   Imprisonment for a couple of days.

＜7・聞く＞

Listening: Announcement

(Narrator) Now you will listen twice to a prerecorded message.

(Woman) 今日はJR東日本を御利用下さいまして、誠に有難うございます。御乗車の皆様に御願いがございます。携帯電話の車内での通話は、他の御客様の御迷惑になりますので、マナーモードに御切り替え願います。また、電車の優先席付近では携帯電話の電源を御切り下さいますよう御願いいたします。御客様の御理解と御協力を御願いいたします。

(Narrator) Now listen again.

(Woman) (Repeat.)

<7・聞く> * Correct answer

Listening: Announcement

(Narrator) Now answer the questions for this selection.

1. Where is this announcement being made?
   (A) on a bus
   (B) on a train *
   (C) in a restaurant
   (D) in a concert hall

2. What is this announcement asking its audience to do?
   (A) To turn off their cellular phones in the special designated seating area. *
   (B) To turn off their cellular phones inside the building.
   (C) To turn off their cellular phones as soon as they get on the train.
   (D) To turn off their cellular phones near the doors.

<8・聞く>

Listening: School Debate

(Narrator) Now you will listen once to a school debate.

(Woman A) それでは、これから生徒会主催の討論会を始めたいと思います。今日は、太郎君と花子さんにクローン技術の応用について討論してもらいます。まず、太郎さんからです。お願いします。

(Man) 僕は食べるためのクローン牛は作ってもいいと思います。賛成の理由は、毎日世界の多くの人が食べ物がなくて死んでいるし、これから世界の人口はどんどん増えて、食料不足が心配だからです。

(Woman A) それでは、花子さん、どうぞ。

(Woman B) 私はクローン牛は反対です。食べられる牛が可哀想です。それに、今牛は十分いると思います。

(Woman A) それでは、クローンペットについては、どう考えますか。

(Woman B) 私はクローン牛もクローンペットも絶対に反対です。もちろん、クローン技術を使って、クローン人間を作ることは、絶対に許してはいけません。動物や人の命を、人間が勝手にコントロールしてはいけないと思います。

(Man) 僕は医療の研究のためのクローン動物や人間を作れば、たくさんの病気の人を助けられるから、いいと思います。

(Woman B) それは倫理的ではありません。研究のためにたくさんのクローンを殺さなければなりませんよ。それは、決して許してはいけません。

< 8・聞く (質問) >   * Correct answer

Listening: School Debate

(Narrator)   Now answer the questions for this selection.

1. Which animal does Taro support cloning?
   - (A) cow *
   - (B) sheep
   - (C) pig
   - (D) chicken

2. What is the reason why Taro supports cloning of animals?
   - (A) Cloned animals are cheap to produce.
   - (B) Cloned animals are easy to produce.
   - (C) Cloned animals can survive in any environment.
   - (D) Cloned animals solve the problem of food shortage. *

3. What does Hanako support cloning?
   - (A) cows
   - (B) pets
   - (C) mice
   - (D) She does not support cloning. *

4. What is Hanako's stand on cloning?
   - (A) Clone technology should only be used to support people's lives.
   - (B) Clone technology should only be used to produce more food.
   - (C) Clone technology should only be used to help sick people.
   - (D) Clone technology should not be used. *

5. What is Taro's stand of cloning?
   - (A) Clone technology should only be used to support people's lives. *
   - (B) Clone technology should only be used to produce more food.
   - (C) Clone technology should only be used to help sick people.
   - (D) Clone technology should not be used.

<9・聞く>

Listening: Gifts

(Narrator) Now you will listen once to a report.

(Woman) 日本に住むと日本人の贈り物についての知識を少し理解していた方がいいでしょう。日本では年に二回お世話になっている人に贈り物をする習慣があります。夏のお盆にお中元を、冬の年末にお歳暮を贈ります。贈る相手は、両親が圧倒的に多く、次に親戚、会社の上司などで、友人にはあまり贈らないようです。ある会社の主婦への調査によると、お中元としてもらいたい物ベスト5は、第1位「商品券」第2位「ビール」第3位「洗剤」第4位「コーヒー」第5位「100％果汁飲料」で、お歳暮としてもらいたい商品ベスト5は、第1位「商品券」第2位「ビール」第3位「コーヒー」第4位「産地直送の生鮮食料品」第5位「洗剤」だそうです。商品券はお中元でもお歳暮でももらいたい物の1位になっていますね。贈り物はデパートから直接送ってくれるので、日本人はだいたいデパートで贈り物の買い物をします。

<9・聞く (質問)>   * Correct answer

Listening: Gifts

(Narrator) Now answer the questions for this selection.

1. Which of these is NOT a Japanese gift giving custom?
   - (A) Japanese people give seasonal gifts twice a year.
   - (B) *Ochuugen* is a seasonal gift given in the spring. *
   - (C) *Oseibo* is a seasonal gift given in the winter.
   - (D) Japanese give seasonal gifts to people who take care of them.

2. To whom do Japanese people NOT give seasonal gifts?
   - (A) To their parents.
   - (B) To their relatives.
   - (C) To their friends. *
   - (D) To their bosses at their working place.

3. Which of the following is the most appreciated by Japanese housewives as gifts?
   - (A) Gift certificates *
   - (B) Beer
   - (C) Coffee
   - (D) Laundry soap

4. What item do Japanese housewives give most often as seasonal gifts?
   - (A) Canned fruits
   - (B) Cooking oil
   - (C) Gift certificates *
   - (D) Healthy drinks

5. Why do Japanese people buy seasonal gifts at department stores?
   - (A) Department stores will send them directly to the recipients. *
   - (B) Department store gifts are nicely wrapped.
   - (C) Department store gifts are very economical.
   - (D) Department store gifts are of excellent quality.

<10・聞く>

Listening: American Food

(Narrator) Now you will listen once to a talk.

(Woman) 私は二度ほどアメリカに行った経験があって、その時の食べ物についての印象を話すわね。まあ一口に言って、アメリカ人の食べ物には失望したわ。油料理が多くって、あとは生野菜、それにポテトかパンでしょ。味もなくて、あの時は悲しかったなあ。それに、アメリカ人の食べる量ってものすごいのよ。デザートが必ず出たけど、となりのテーブルに座ったアメリカの男性がケーキの上にアイスクリームをのっけて美味しそうに食べていたのには、正直言ってショックだったわ。あれだけ食べたら、アメリカ人みたいにでっかくなるのは当たり前よ。食材も種類が少ないし、調味料もお塩とこしょうぐらいで、私はお醤油の味が恋しかったわ。不思議に思ったのは、アメリカでサラダに豆があったのよ。日本じゃ豆ってお砂糖で甘くしてあんこなんかにして食べるじゃない。アメリカ人って、豆にはお砂糖を入れないんだってね。ナイフとフォークで両手を使って食べるのって、けっこう疲れて、私はお箸の生活の方が性に合っているわと思ったわ。お箸って便利でしょ。何でも食べられるから。日本じゃ、お茶碗とかお椀とか手で持って食べるけど、フォークを使ってお皿からライスを食べると食べた気がしなかったな。でも、パンだけは美味しかったな。パンはいろいろな種類があって焼きたてだったから、温かくて美味しかった。従業員のサービスには感心出来なかったし、チップをあげなきゃいけないのも腹立ったし、第一計算がめんどうで、嫌だったな。中華料理のレストランを探しあてた時には、ごはんが食べられると思って、本当に嬉しかったの。日本に帰って何を食べたかったと思う？うどんとラーメン。あのおつゆが本当に恋しかったよ。

<10・聞く(質問)>   * Correct answer

Listening: American Food

(Narrator) Now answer the questions for this selection.

1. What food did this person enjoy when she ate at a restaurant in America?
   (A) steak
   (B) potatoes
   (C) salad
   (D) bread *

2. What surprised this person the most at the restaurant she went to in America?
   (A) An American man was eating a cake with ice cream. *
   (B) An American family was eating lots of food.
   (C) American children were eating a big cake.
   (D) Everyone was eating a big meal.

3. What food was strange to this person when she ate at a restaurant in America?
   (A) sweet beans
   (B) unsweetened beans *
   (C) cake with ice cream
   (D) baked potato

4. When this person returned to Japan, what food did she want to eat the most?
   (A) sushi
   (B) white rice
   (C) noodle soup *
   (D) miso soup

5. What kind of opinion does this person have about dining at American restaurants?
   (A) The workers at American restaurants are kind.
   (B) American restaurants should offer chopsticks.
   (C) Leaving a tip at the restaurant is reasonable.
   (D) Eating with a knife and fork is harder than eating with chopsticks. *

<11・聞く>

Listening: Department Store Telephone Message

(Narrator)　Now you will listen twice to a prerecorded message.

(Woman)　こちらは池袋の桜デパートでございます。本日月曜日は定休日でございます。当店の営業時間は午前9時30分から午後8時までとなっております。4月10日、月曜日まで、8階の催し会場では、新学期のご準備のための特別セールを実施しております。また、地下1階、食料品売り場では、ただいま、各地で有名なお花見弁当を取り揃えております。新鮮で美味しいカニやエビなどを使った北海道弁当など、いろいろございます。なお食料品売り場は7時までの販売となっております。ご来店をお待ち申し上げております。

(Narrator)　Now listen again.

(Woman)　(Repeat.)

<11・聞く (質問)>   * Correct answer

Listening: Department Store Telephone Message

(Narrator)   Now answer the questions for this selection.

1. When is this department store closed?
   (A) Sundays
   (B) Mondays *
   (C) Tuesdays
   (D) Thursdays

2. What are the business hours at this department store?
   (A) 7:30 a.m. to 7:00 p.m.
   (B) 8:30 a.m. to 8:00 p.m.
   (C) 9:00 a.m. to 7:00 p.m.
   (D) 9:30 a.m. to 8:00 p.m. *

3. What special sale does this department store now have?
   (A) A back to school sale *
   (B) A New Year sale
   (C) An end of the year sale
   (D) A spring fashion sale

4. What is on sale at the food corner?
   (A) Seafood bento sale
   (B) Hokkaido bento sale
   (C) Bento from various regions
   (D) Bento from various regions celebrating cherry blossom viewing *

5. Which of the following information is correct about this department store?
   (A) The special event corner is located on the 7th floor.
   (B) The special event corner will end on Monday, April 10th. *
   (C) The food corner is located on the second floor of the basement.
   (D) The food corner closes at 6:00 p.m.

スクリプトと答・聞

<12・聞く>

Listening: Four Seasons

(Narrator) Now you will listen twice to an announcement.

(Woman) 日本は縦に長い島国ですから、気候は、季節によっても場所によってもかなり違います。日本の四季はそれぞれに美しく、観光の目的によって、適切な季節を選ぶことをお勧めします。桜の下でお花見をしたい方は、春の4月上旬ごろでしょう。桜前線は南からだんだん北に移って行きます。京都ではだいたい4月の初め頃に行けば見られるはずですが、年によっても違います。日本は6月ごろから7月半ばにかけて梅雨という雨の季節になります。毎日朝から晩まで雨がしとしと降って、湿度も高いです。傘が必要な季節ですから、旅行にはちょっと大変です。日本の夏は蒸し暑く、汗がよく出ます。秋になるとまた過ごしやすくなりますが、台風も多い季節です。晩秋になると、紅葉が素晴らしいです。日本の冬は寒いです。二月初めの札幌の雪祭り、有名です。雪と氷で作られる像は百以上もあります。四季の日本の美しさをぜひ味わっていただきたいです。

(Narrator) Now listen again.

(Woman) (Repeat.)

<12・聞く (質問)>　　＊ Correct answer

Listening: *Four Seasons*

(Narrator)　Now answer the questions for this selection.

1. Which is INCORRECT description of Japan?
   (A) Japan is a horizontally long island. ＊
   (B) The climate of Japan differs considerably by season.
   (C) The climate of Japan differs considerably by location.
   (D) The four seasons of Japan are all beautiful in their own ways.

2. Which is an INCORRECT description of cherry blossoms in Japan?
   (A) Cherry blossoms bloom in early April.
   (B) Cherry blossoms start to bloom from southern Japan to northern Japan.
   (C) In Kyoto, Cherry blossoms bloom around the end of April. ＊
   (D) The cherry blossom season differs from year to year.

3. Which is an INCORRECT description of the rainy season in Japan?
   (A) The rainy season starts around June.
   (B) The rainy season ends around the middle of July.
   (C) During the rainy season, it rains very hard all day long. ＊
   (D) During the rainy season, it rains lightly all day long.

4. Which is an INCORRECT description of summer and autumn in Japan?
   (A) Summer in Japan is very hot and humid.
   (B) Typhoons come to Japan mostly during the summer. ＊
   (C) Autumn in Japan is comfortable.
   (D) The autumn colors are beautiful.

5. Which is an INCORRECT description of winter in Japan?
   (A) The Snow Festival is held in Sapporo.
   (B) The Snow Festival is held in the beginning of February.
   (C) The statues at the festival are made of snow and ice.
   (D) There are more than a thousand statues at the Snow Festival. ＊

<13・聞く>

Listening: Elections

(Narrator) Now you will listen once to a conversation.

(Woman) ケンは、選挙に出たことがある？

(Man) 僕は高校一年生の時に、生徒会の会長に立候補して、その時は選挙に負けてしまったよ。でも、二年生の時に、もう一度挑戦して、みごと当選。その結果を知った時は、本当に嬉しかったよ。

(Woman) そう、すごいね。私は投票はするけど、立候補したことはないわ。

(Man) まりは、政治に関心がある？日本は特に、女性の政治家が少ないらしいね。なぜかなあ。女性が政治に関心を持たないと、日本の社会は男性の意見で決められてしまうよ。

(Woman) そうね。ケンは将来、政治家になりたいと思う？

(Man) さあ、今よく分からないよ。でも、僕の専門の環境問題は、政治によって、悪くなったり良くなったりするからねえ。僕はゴア元副大統領の地球温暖化の映画を見て、民主党とか共和党とか言ってる場合じゃないと思ったよ。

(Woman) 私も自分の国のことだけでなく、地球全体のことを考えられる政治家を支持するわ。

＜13・聞く＞   * Correct answer

Listening: Elections

(Narrator)   Now answer the questions for this selection.

1. What is Ken's experience with elections?
   (A)   Ken never ran in an elction.
   (B)   Ken was successful at his first run for office.
   (C)   Ken was successful at his second run for office. *
   (D)   Ken was successful in every election.

2. What is Mari's experience with elections?
   (A)   Mari never ran for office. *
   (B)   Mari never voted in elections.
   (C)   Mari once ran for office, but she was not elected.
   (D)   Mari was once elected as a student body officer.

3. What is Ken's opinion about Japanese politics?
   (A)   More women should become interested in politics. *
   (B)   Japanese politics are changing a lot.
   (C)   Japanese voters should decide on their prime minister by direct election.
   (D)   Japan should cooperate more with the rest of Asia.

4. What opinion does Ken express in this selection?
   (A)   Ken wants to become a politician.
   (B)   Ken thinks politics influences decisions on environmental issues. *
   (C)   Ken supports the Republican party.
   (D)   Ken thinks that Mr. Gore should become president.

5. What opinion does Mari have?
   (A)   Mari thinks that more women should run for political office.
   (B)   Mari favors politicians who support poor people.
   (C)   Mari supports persons who thinks globally. *
   (D)   Mari thinks that she should run for political office.

スクリプトと答・聞

<1・読む(質問)>   * Correct answer

Reading: Web Interview Article

(Narrator)   Now answer the questions for this selection.

1. What is Mrs. Peterson's educational background?
   (A) She graduated from a university in Hawaii and then a university in Kyoto.
   (B) She graduated from a university in Osaka.
   (C) She graduated from the University of Hawaii with a major in foreign language education. *
   (D) She majored in art at a university in Kyoto.

2. What is an accurate description of Mrs. Peterson's life?
   (A) Before she could not understand English, but now she does not have any problems with English.
   (B) She is enjoying her family and friends, but has a little problem with her job.
   (C) She feels lucky to have a good life. *
   (D) She is still nervous about meeting people of different ethnicities.

3. What does Mrs. Peterson recommend to visitors to Hawaii?
   (A) People should visit the famous tourist attractions.
   (B) People should take a city bus tour.
   (C) People should visit the shopping center.
   (D) People should walk around the city. *

4. What kind of restaurants and dishes does Mrs. Peterson enjoy?
   (A) She likes sushi at Japanese restaurants.
   (B) She likes noodles at Japanese restaurants.
   (C) She likes the green curry dishes at Thai restaurants. *
   (D) She likes the green papaya salads at Thai restaurants.

5. What does Mrs. Peterson enjoy?
   (A) She enjoys fishing.
   (B) She enjoys snorkeling. *
   (C) She enjoys swimming in pools.
   (D) She enjoys surfing.

<2・読む(質問)>   *Correct answer

Reading: *Magazine Article*

(Narrator)   Now answer the questions for this selection.

1. According to the article, why did Ms. Yamamura always feel inferior?
   (A) She could not compete with her sister's achievements. *
   (B) Her sister was very mean to her.
   (C) She was bullied in school.
   (D) Her teacher treated her as an inferior.

2. How did she gain confidence?
   (A) She excelled in sports.
   (B) Her grades improved.
   (C) She became popular with boys.
   (D) Her talent in art was recognized. *

3. Why did she break up with her boyfriend when she was in the 11th grade?
   (A) Her mother didn't like him.
   (B) He developed an interest in her best friend. *
   (C) She met someone else and she liked her new boyfriend better.
   (D) She was more interested in painting than in her boyfriend.

4. What is her new challenge?
   (A) To draw human figures.
   (B) To draw flowers.
   (C) To paint natural scenery. *
   (D) To draw animals and birds.

5. What benefits did she gain from painting?
   (A) She was recognized by her school friends.
   (B) She found true joy in painting. *
   (C) She was able to make her family happy.
   (D) She could find a better job.

< 3・読む (質問) >   * Correct answer

Reading: Letter

(Narrator)   Now answer the questions for this selection.

1. What year of college is Erin in now?
    (A)   Erin is a first semester freshman at MIT.
    (B)   Erin is a second semester freshman at MIT. *
    (C)   Erin is a sophomore at MIT.
    (D)   Erin is a junior at MIT.

2. What kind of trip to Japan did Erin experience?
    (A)   Erin's trip was a prize she won at the Japan Bowl state tournament.
    (B)   Erin went to Japan with a teammate and her teacher.
    (C)   Erin visited Tokyo first.
    (D)   Erin visited Hiroshima first. *

3. What happened in Hiroshima?
    (A)   Erin stayed at her teacher's brother's house. *
    (B)   Erin bought the book "Fire Bird" at the bookstore.
    (C)   Erin read ten volumes of a book titled "Fire Bird."
    (D)   Erin was interviewed by a NHK news caster in English at the Peace Park.

4. Which of the following does NOT describe Erin's interests?
    (A)   Erin is interested in Japanese traditional culture. *
    (B)   Erin is curious about robots.
    (C)   Erin loves to play Japanese computer games.
    (D)   Erin likes green tea shaved ice.

5. Why did this teacher write a letter to Erin?
    (A)   The robot reminded this teacher of Erin.
    (B)   The "Fire Bird" anime reminded this teacher of Erin. *
    (C)   Erin visited this teacher at school, but her teacher was not in.
    (D)   This teacher heard that Erin is returning home for summer.

<4・読む(質問)>   * Correct answer

Reading: *My Hashi*

(Narrator)   Now answer the questions for this selection.

1. Who started promoting the practice of carrying one's own chopsticks?
    (A)   A group of students
    (B)   A group of teachers
    (C)   A group of parents
    (D)   A group of citizens *

2. What benefits do restaurant customers get by using their own chopsticks?
    (A)   The customers can get free chopsticks.
    (B)   The customers can get a free cup of coffee. *
    (C)   The customers can get a discount coupon for the next visit.
    (D)   The customers can get a free package of tissues.

3. How do the participating restaurant owners benefit?
    (A)   The restaurants receive publicity in the newspaper.
    (B)   The restaurants receive publicity in the promotion group's magazine. *
    (C)   The restaurants will be recognized by the city.
    (D)   The restaurants will be recognized on a radio program.

4. What is the public's reaction to this movement?
    (A)   More people started to use their own chopsticks at the restaurants. *
    (B)   So far 40 people have used their own chopsticks at the restaurants.
    (C)   Restaurant owners didn't support this movement.
    (D)   People often forget to carry their own chopsticks.

5. Who wrote this article?
    (A)   A professional newspaper reporter wrote this article.
    (B)   A senior citizen wrote this article.
    (C)   A junior high school student wrote this article. *
    (D)   A high school student wrote this article.

< 5・読む(質問) >   * Correct answer

Reading: *International Exchange*

(Narrator)   Now answer the questions for this selection.

1. What kind of school is Yuuhigaoka High School?
   - (A)   It is a co-ed public high school. *
   - (B)   It is a co-ed private high school.
   - (C)   It is a music high school.
   - (D)   It is a very traditional girls' school.

2. Which of the following correctly describes Yuuhigaoka High School?
   - (A)   It's near the Kansai Airport, so it is a little noisy.
   - (B)   It has wonderful facilities such as a concert hall and a pool, but they are in a tall building. *
   - (C)   It has a school excursion to Korea and China.
   - (D)   It has an English study tour to England and a music study tour to Vienna.

3. Which of the following is true about the teleconferencing project with Yuuhigaoka High School?
   - (A)   It will happen two times a year with 40 Yuuhigaoka students.
   - (B)   One of the goals is for Yuuhigaoka to use traditional Japanese musical instruments.
   - (C)   One of the goals is to create a Japanese graduation song for our school. *
   - (D)   Yuuhigaoka students compose the lyrics and we compose the music for a graduation song.

4. Which of the following is NOT true about the series of teleconferencing sessions?
   - (A)   For the first teleconference, we introduce ourselves.
   - (B)   For the second teleconference, we will discuss a musical piece.
   - (C)   For the third teleconference, we will have a presentation.
   - (D)   For our Japanese graduation, Yuuhigaoka students will play the song for us from Japan. *

5. What kind of technology will NOT be used by the students for this project?
   - (A)   We will NOT use the internet.
   - (B)   We will NOT use Skype. *
   - (C)   We will NOT use our laptops.
   - (D)   We will NOT use cellular phones.

< 6・読む(質問)> ＊ Correct answer

Reading: E-mails

(Narrator) Now answer the questions for this selection.

1. Which message is from someone who cannot go to the art museum?
    (A) Message # 1
    (B) Message # 2
    (C) Message # 4 ＊
    (D) Message # 6

2. In which of the classes below will there be an exam tomorrow?
    (A) history
    (B) math
    (C) literature
    (D) economics ＊

3. Why was soccer practice canceled?
    (A) The weather was bad. ＊
    (B) The coach was injured.
    (C) There is an important exam on the next day.
    (D) The coach caught a cold.

4. Who has the blue and white umbrella now?
    (A) Mari
    (B) The receiver of the e-mail
    (C) Erika
    (D) Tomoko ＊

5. Which message conveys an encouraging message to the receiver?
    (A) Message # 3
    (B) Message # 4
    (C) Message # 5 ＊
    (D) Message # 6

< 7・読む (質問) >　　＊ Correct answer

Reading: Cellular Phones

(Narrator)　Now answer the questions for this selection.

1. What is Keiko's favorite cellular phone mode?
   (A) Her favorite is the alarm mode. ＊
   (B) Her favorite is the shopping mode.
   (C) Her favorite is the camera mode.
   (D) Her favorite is the train timetable mode.

2. When did Keiko shop on the internet?
   (A) Keiko shopped on the net auction last night and made a payment last night.
   (B) Keiko shopped on the net auction this morning and made a payment this morning.
   (C) Keiko shopped on the net auction last night and made a payment this morning. ＊
   (D) Keiko shopped on the net auction last night and is going to pay later.

3. How does Keiko pay for the cellular phone?
   (A) Keiko is charged for every message sent, but is not charged for received messages.
   (B) Keiko is charged for every received message, but is not charged for sending messages.
   (C) Keiko is charged for every message sent and received.
   (D) Keiko is charged a fixed rate for both sending and receiving messages. ＊

4. Where did Keiko meet her friend, and what did they do?
   (A) Keiko met her friend on her way to the university and they walked to the university together.
   (B) Keiko met her friend on her way to the university and they took a photo together.
   (C) Keiko met her friend on her way home and they went to a convenience store together.
   (D) Keiko met her friend on her way home and they took a photo together. ＊

5. What did Keiko not do last evening before she went to bed?
   (A) Keiko updated her blog. ＊
   (B) Keiko set her alarm.
   (C) Keiko talked to her boyfriend.
   (D) Keiko checked the train schedule to Shibuya.

< 8・読む(質問) >   ＊ Correct answer

Reading: Article

(Narrator)   Now answer the questions for this selection.

1. Which of the following descriptions of NEET is NOT correct?
   (A) The word NEET originated in Japan. ＊
   (B) NEETs do not work.
   (C) NEETs do not attend school.
   (D) NEETs do not take vocational training.

2. Which statement about NEETs is NOT correct?
   (A) There were about 65,000 NEETs in Japan in 2003. ＊
   (B) About 2% of the young population can be categorized as NEET.
   (C) In some areas of England, as many as 15〜25% of the young population are NEETs.
   (D) The NEET problem in England is more serious than in Japan.

3. What description of freeters is NOT correct?
   (A) The freeters change their jobs often.
   (B) The word "freeter" was made in Japan.
   (C) There are about 200,000 freeters in Japan. ＊
   (D) About 7% of the young population in Japan are considered to be freeters.

4. What is NOT given as a reason for companies who favor hiring freeters?
   (A) The company does not have to pay a large salary to freeters.
   (B) The company does not have to cover insurance for freeters.
   (C) The company can fire freeters any time.
   (D) The company does not have to train freeters. ＊

5. Which statement accurately describes the situation for NEETs and freeters?
   (A) The number of NEETs and freeters is gradually increasing. ＊
   (B) The number of NEETs and freeters is rapidly increasing.
   (C) The number of NEETs and freeters is gradually decreasing.
   (D) The number of NEETs and freeters is rapidly decreasing.

< 9・読む(質問) >   * Correct answer

Reading: Jobs

(Narrator) Now answer the questions for this selection.

1. What is the minimum number of hours this supermarket requires their applicants to work?
   - (A) 4 hours
   - (B) 10 hours
   - (C) 12 hours *
   - (D) Not specified

2. Which benefit is NOT included?
   - (A) Mini bonus
   - (B) Transportation stipend
   - (C) Uniform
   - (D) Boarding *

3. What is the difference between conditions for minors and adults?
   - (A) Working time
   - (B) Wages *
   - (C) Promotion
   - (D) There is no difference.

4. What type of person is this supermarket looking for?
   - (A) Motivated *
   - (B) Well-desciplined
   - (C) Intelligent
   - (D) Healthy

5. What does the supermarket suggest to interested applicants?
   - (A) Send a resume by mail
   - (B) Walk-in
   - (C) Telephone *
   - (D) All of the above

<10・読む(質問)>   * Correct answer

Reading: Resume (2 pages)

(Narrator) Now answer the questions for this selection.

1. Where did Ken attend elementary school?
   - (A) Palo Alto
   - (B) Honolulu *
   - (C) Tokyo
   - (D) Kyoto

2. Based on Ken's resume, which statement is NOT correct?
   - (A) Ken graduated from a public middle school.
   - (B) Ken graduated from a private high school.
   - (C) Ken graduated from Stanford University. *
   - (D) Ken had an internship during his college life.

3. What special qualification does Ken NOT have?
   - (A) lifeguard license *
   - (B) 4th level of *kanji* proficiency
   - (C) 2nd level of Japanese proficiency
   - (D) driver's license

4. What is NOT a correct description of Ken?
   - (A) Ken likes science and mathematics. *
   - (B) Ken's hobbies are reading and cooking.
   - (C) Ken belonged to the basketball club.
   - (D) Ken is very healthy.

5. What kind of job does Ken want to do?
   - (A) Ken wants to work in engineering.
   - (B) Ken wants to work for a publishing company.
   - (C) Ken wants to work in international business.
   - (D) Ken wants to work on environmental issues. *

<11・読む(質問)>   *Correct answer

Reading: Invitation Letter

(Narrator) Now answer the questions for this selection.

1. What event is this invitation for?
   (A) funeral
   (B) wedding *
   (C) birthday party
   (D) anniversary

2. When is this event?
   (A) May 20th
   (B) May 23rd
   (C) June 23rd *
   (D) May 30th

3. Where will this event be held?
   (A) Sunshine Hotel in Kyoto
   (B) Orchid Hotel in Shinjuku
   (C) Orchid Restaurant in Tokyo
   (D) Orchid Room of the Sunshine Hotel in Shinjuku *

4. What is the setting for this event?
   (A) The ceremony will be held at a church.
   (B) The ceremony will be held in front of the participants. *
   (C) The party will be held at the hotel garden.
   (D) The party will be held at a restaurant in the hotel.

5. What is this letter requesting?
   (A) Not to bring flowers.
   (B) To respond by May 30th. *
   (C) Not to give money.
   (D) To attend the event in casual attire.

<12・読む(質問)> * Correct answer

Reading: Cherry Blossom

(Narrator) Now answer the questions for this selection.

1. What kinds of themes are used in songs associated with cherry blossoms?
    (A) Love and memories
    (B) Separation and happiness
    (C) Separation and new beginnings *
    (D) Youth and friendship

2. In what season do cherry blossoms bloom in Japan?
    (A) Generally between the end of March and the middle of April
    (B) Generally between the beginning of March and the end of April
    (C) About the same time as the school graduation ceremony and the new school year. *
    (D) About the same time as Golden Week.

3. What activites do Japanese people enjoy outdoors while they view cherry blossoms?
    (A) Singing *karaoke*
    (B) Drinking sake
    (C) Having a tea ceremony
    (D) All of the above *

4. What characteristic of cherry blossoms has attracted Japanese people?
    (A) The elegance of cherry blossoms
    (B) The short life span of cherry blossoms *
    (C) The beautiful color of cherry blossoms
    (D) That they are a symbol of new life

5. What does the writer want to say in this article?
    (A) People can achieve success by enduring hardships.
    (B) People can be happy when they work together well.
    (C) The cherry blossom season brings happiness to people.
    (D) People who live a short life appreciate their lives most. *

<13・読む(質問)>   *Correct answer

Reading: Article

(Narrator) Now answer the questions for this selection.

1. What is this article about?
   (A) The natural environment should be protected.
   (B) Recycling is important.
   (C) Energy is a big issue.
   (D) Global warming is a very serious problem. *

2. What is NOT related to global warming?
   (A) Glaciers will melt and the sea level will rise.
   (B) We will have more forest fires.
   (C) We will have more earthquakes. *
   (D) Food will become scarce.

3. What is true about the Kyoto Protocol?
   (A) According to the survey, Japan produced the third most CO_2 of all the countries in the world.
   (B) The Kyoto Protocol was established in order to solve global warming. *
   (C) America supported the Kyoto Protocol.
   (D) The Kyoto Protocol was established in 2002.

4. What did the writer decide to do?
   (A) The writer decided to buy a hybrid car.
   (B) The writer decided to use less gasoline. *
   (C) The writer decided to use public transportation.
   (D) The writer decided to walk more.

5. What did the writer suggest to the readers?
   (A) We should change our values and what it means to have a rich life. *
   (B) We should use less energy.
   (C) We should educate people more about sustainability.
   (D) We should recycle more.

<14・読む (質問)> * Correct answer

Reading: Sweets

(Narrator) Now answer the questions for this selection.

1. What kind of sweets does this menu offer?
   (A) maple leaf shaped sweets *
   (B) plum flower shaped sweets
   (C) fan shaped sweets
   (D) peach shaped sweets

2. Which flavor of sweets is NOT listed?
   (A) green tea
   (B) chocolate
   (C) coffee *
   (D) red bean paste

3. What flavor of sweets do they NOT have in the spring?
   (A) strawberry cheese
   (B) lemon cheese *
   (C) blueberry cheese
   (D) yogurt cheese

4. What can you order for 90 yen at this shop?
   (A) one regular sweet and a cup of tea including tax
   (B) one cheese flavored sweet and a cup of tea excluding tax
   (C) one regular sweet and a cup of tea excluding tax
   (D) one cheese flavored sweet and a cup of tea including tax *

5. Which special note appears on this menu?
   (A) You must pay after eating.
   (B) You must pay before eating. *
   (C) Only cheese flavored spring sweets are freshly baked.
   (D) Only regular sweets offered all year long are freshly baked.

<15・読む(質問)>   ＊ Correct answer

Reading: Travel Guide

(Narrator) Now answer the questions for this selection.

1. What kind of tour does this travel guide introduce?
   (A) Visiting famous temples
   (B) A city tour
   (C) Climbing famous mountains
   (D) Walking historical mountain paths ＊

2. When is this tour available?
   (A) Weekdays between April 1st and September 30th
   (B) Weekends between April 1st and September 30th
   (C) Weekends between April 1st and September 30th except on three days ＊
   (D) All weekdays and May 6th, August 12th and 13th

3. What is included in the tour fee?
   (A) Taxi or bus fare
   (B) Snacks ＊
   (C) Lunch
   (D) Bathing in a hot spring

4. Which of the following is NOT correct?
   (A) The meeting time is 9:00 a.m.
   (B) The departure time is 9:15 a.m.
   (C) Lunch time is around 1:45 p.m.
   (D) The return time is 3:00 p.m. ＊

5. Which of the following is correct?
   (A) One should wear comfortable shoes. ＊
   (B) The maximum number of people taken on this tour is six.
   (C) In case of light rain, the tour will be canceled.
   (D) The cost of the tour is different for adults and children.

<1・話す（会話）>

15点
20秒×4

Conversation: Host Mother

You will participate in a simulated conversation. Each time it is your turn to speak, you will have 20 seconds to record. You should respond as fully and as appropriately as possible.

You will introduce yourself in a conversation with Mrs. Kondo, the mother of your Japanese host family.

(Host mother)　はじめまして。近藤です。よろしくね。

(20 seconds)

(Host mother)　どんな事をするのが好き？趣味は？

(20 seconds)

(Host mother)　食事とかで何か嫌いな物とか、ぜったい食べられない物とかあったら、教えておいてね。

(20 seconds)

(Host mother)　日本で何かこれだけはしてみたいとかいう希望を教えて。

(20 seconds)

スクリプト：会話

＜２・話す（会話）＞

15点
20秒 x 4

Conversation: Sports

You will participate in a simulated conversation. Each time it is your turn to speak, you will have 20 seconds to record. You should respond as fully and as appropriately as possible.

You will introduce yourself in a conversation with Mr. Ito, a newspaper reporter from Japan.

(Male reporter) 初めまして。スポーツ新聞の伊藤ですが、今日はスポーツの部活について、インタビューしますので、よろしくお願いします。

(20 seconds)

(Male reporter) どんなスポーツをしていますか。なぜですか。

(20 seconds)

(Male reporter) そうですか。勉強とスポーツとどちらの方が大事だと思いますか。なぜですか。

(20 seconds)

(Male reporter) そうですか。では、最後に高校生に人気があるスポーツについて教えて下さい。

(20 seconds)

スクリプト：会話

＜３・話す（会話）＞

Conversation: Home

15点
20秒 x 4

You will participate in a simulated conversation. Each time it is your turn to speak, you will have 20 seconds to record. You should respond as fully and as appropriately as possible.

You will have a conversation with Daisuke Kato, a Japanese student who is going to stay in your house.

(Male student)　　初めまして。来月からお宅に一カ月お世話になる加藤です。
　　　　　　　　よろしくお願いします。

(20 seconds)

(Male student)　　すみませんが、どんなうちに住んでいるんですか。

(20 seconds)

(Male student)　　そうですか。うちは便利な所にあるんですか。

(20 seconds)

(Male student)　　あ、そうですか。うちで家事を手伝わなきゃいけないとか
　　　　　　　　門限（げん）とかほかの規則（きそく）があったら、教えて下さい。

(20 seconds)

スクリプト：会話

<4・話す（会話）>

15点
20秒 x 4

Conversation: Recycling

You will participate in a simulated conversation. Each time it is your turn to speak, you will have 20 seconds to record. You should respond as fully and as appropriately as possible.

You will have a conversation with Dr. Kawano, a professor from a Japanese university.

| (Professor) | 初めまして。川野です。今日は環境問題について質問します。どうぞよろしく。 |

(20 seconds)

| (Professor) | まず、どこでどんなリサイクルをしていますか。 |

(20 seconds)

| (Professor) | そうですか。リサイクルについてどう思いますか。意見を教えて下さい。 |

(20 seconds)

| (Professor) | そうですか。それでは、今リサイクルについて、どんな問題がありますか。 |

(20 seconds)

＜５・話す（会話）＞

Conversation: School

15点
20秒 x 4

You will participate in a simulated conversation. Each time it is your turn to speak, you will have 20 seconds to record. You should respond as fully and as appropriately as possible.

You will have a conversation with Mr. Yamamura, the father of your Japanese host family.

(Host father)　初めまして。山村です。どうぞよろしく。学校についていろいろ質問してもいい？

(20 seconds)

(Host father)　アメリカの学校は何時に始まって、何時に終わるんですか。放課後（ほうか）はたいてい何をしているんですか。

(20 seconds)

(Host father)　そうですか。学校に制服があるんですか。制服について、どう思う？

(20 seconds)

(Host father)　そう？好きな科目は何？なぜ？

(20 seconds)

スクリプト：会話

<6・話す（会話）>

Conversation: Fashion

15点
20秒 x 4

You will participate in a simulated conversation. Each time it is your turn to speak, you will have 20 seconds to record. You should respond as fully and as appropriately as possible.

You will have a telephone conversation with Mai, a Japanese student.

(Female Student)　　初めまして。舞です。今日のトピックはファッションです。どうぞよろしく。

(20 seconds)

(Female Student)　　まず、今どんなファッションが流行っていますか。

(20 seconds)

(Female Student)　　あなたはどんな服装や髪型が好きですか。なぜですか。

(20 seconds)

(Female Student)　　日本のファッションについて何か質問して下さい。

(20 seconds)

＜７・話す（会話）＞

Conversation: Cellular Phones

15点
20秒 x 4

You will participate in a simulated conversation. Each time it is your turn to speak, you will have 20 seconds to record. You should respond as fully and as appropriately as possible.

You will have a conversation with Kyoko, a student from Japan.

(Student)　　　初めまして。京子です。どんな携帯を持っていますか。

(20 seconds)

(Student)　　　そうですか。一ヶ月いくらぐらい払っていますか。

(20 seconds)

(Student)　　　そうですか。携帯は何のために使っていますか。

(20 seconds)

(Student)　　　そうですか。何か日本の携帯について質問がありますか。

(20 seconds)

スクリプト：会話

<8・話す（会話）>

Conversation: Job

15点
20秒 x 4

You will participate in a simulated conversation. Each time it is your turn to speak, you will have 20 seconds to record. You should respond as fully and as appropriately as possible.

You will have a conversation with Mrs. Nakata, an interviewer from a Japanese radio station.

(Interviewer)　初めまして。サクララジオの山田です。先日は、アンケートにお答え下さいまして、ありがとうございました。

(20 seconds)

(Interviewer)　アンケートについてもう少し詳しく教えて下さい。仕事を選ぶ時に、給料と仕事の内容と、どちらの方が大切だと思いますか。

(20 seconds)

(Interviewer)　それはどうしてですか。

(20 seconds)

(Interviewer)　あ、そうですか。それから、今度うちのラジオ局に来て、高校生の将来の夢についてもっと話していただけるでしょうか。

(20 seconds)

< 9・話す（会話）>

15点
20秒 x 4

Conversation: Christmas

You will participate in a simulated conversation. Each time it is your turn to speak, you will have 20 seconds to record. You should respond as fully and as appropriately as possible.

You will have a conversation with Mrs. Nakamura, the mother of your Japanese host family.

(Host mother)　クリスマスは、いつもどう過ごしているの？

(20 seconds)

(Host mother)　あ、そう？じゃ、クリスマスの前には、どんなことをするの？

(20 seconds)

(Host mother)　そう？クリスマスプレゼントは、だれにどんなものをあげるの？いくらぐらい？

(20 seconds)

(Host mother)　クリスマスプレゼントをあげる習慣についてどう思うか、聞かせて。

(20 seconds)

スクリプト：会話

<10・話す（会話）>

15点
20秒 x 4

Conversation: Commuting to School

You will participate in a simulated conversation. Each time it is your turn to speak, you will have 20 seconds to record. You should respond as fully and as appropriately as possible.

You will have a conversation with Mr. Nakamura, a Japanese school newspaper writer, about commuting to school.

(Man)　　　初めまして。花山高校新聞部の中村と申します。どうぞよろしく御願いします。今日はそちらの通学についていろいろ教えて下さい。

(20 seconds)

(Man)　　　毎日、生徒は何で通学していますか。

(20 seconds)

(Man)　　　そうですか。そちらの町の通勤通学で一番の問題点は何でしょうか。

(20 seconds)

(Man)　　　今日はお手伝い下さりどうもありがとうございました。では、日本の通勤通学について何か質問があったら、どうぞ。

(20 seconds)

スクリプト：会話

<11・話す（会話）>

15点
20秒 x 4

Conversation: Souvenir Shopping

You will participate in a simulated conversation. Each time it is your turn to speak, you will have 20 seconds to record. You should respond as fully and as appropriately as possible.

You will have a conversation with a Japanese customer at the souvenir shop where you are working.

(Customer)   すみません、お土産をさがしているんですが、何か安くてかわいい物がありますか。

(20 seconds)

(Customer)   ああ、いいですね。いくらですか。たくさん買ったら、割引がありますか。

(20 seconds)

(Customer)   ああ、いいですね。あのう、お土産なので、きれいに包装（ほうそう）してもらえませんか。

(20 seconds)

(Customer)   ありがとうございます。あのう、日本のブログにのせたいので、何かお店の事、教えて下さい。

(20 seconds)

スクリプト：会話

<12・話す（会話）>

15点
20秒 x 4

Conversation: An Injury

You will participate in a simulated conversation. Each time it is your turn to speak, you will have 20 seconds to record. You should respond as fully and as appropriately as possible.

You have fractured your arm in Japan and you will have a conversation with Mr. Tsuda, a Japanese teacher at Japanese host school.

(Teacher)　　腕(うで)にギブスをしているけど、どうしたんですか。

(20 seconds)

(Teacher)　　そうですか。今、大丈夫ですか。

(20 seconds)

(Teacher)　　治るまで、どのぐらいかかるんですか。

(20 seconds)

(Teacher)　　そうですか。何か手伝えることがありますか。

(20 seconds)

スクリプト：会話

<13・話す（会話）>

Conversation: Japan Trip

15点
20秒 x 4

You will participate in a simulated conversation. Each time it is your turn to speak, you will have 20 seconds to record. You should respond as fully and as appropriately as possible.

You will have a conversation with Mr. Okada, a Japanese visitor at your school.

(Visitor)　　　　初めまして。岡田です。日本語が上手ですねえ。日本へ行ったことがあるんですか。

(20 seconds)

(Visitor)　　　　そうですか。日本でお寺や神社を見物することに興味がありますか。

(20 seconds)

(Visitor)　　　　そうですか。じゃ、旅館に泊まるのとホテルに泊まるのと、どちらの方がいいと思いますか。

(20 seconds)

(Visitor)　　　　そうですか。日本に行けたら、何を一番してみたいですか。

(20 seconds)

スクリプト：会話

＜１・話す（留守番電話）＞

15点
20秒 x 4

Return Telephone Call: Welcome Party

You will participate in a simulated telephone conversation with someone you are calling back after receiving a message. First, you will listen to the voice message. Then the telephone call will begin. Each time it is your turn to speak, you will have 20 seconds to record. You should respond as fully and as appropriately as possible.

(Narrator)　　Listen to the voice message.

(Woman)　　もしもし、留学センターの鈴木です。今晩の留学生の歓迎会についてなんですが、ちょっと問題がありまして、至急お電話下さい。

(Narrator)　　Now the telephone call will begin. After the phone is answered, begin with a greeting and then explain why you are calling.

(Woman)　　[Telephone] [Rings twice and picks up] もしもし、留学センターの鈴木ですが。

(20 seconds)

(Woman)　　今晩の留学生の歓迎会なんですが、時間が変更になったんですよ。

(20 seconds)

(Woman)　　それに、実は、車で迎えに行くつもりでしたが、車がこわれて行けなくなってしまったんです。どうしましょうか。

(20 seconds)

(Woman)　　そうですか。では、よろしくお願いします。

(20 seconds)

スクリプト：留守番電話

<2・話す（留守番電話）>

Return Telephone Call: Breaking a Date

15点
20秒 x 4

You will participate in a simulated telephone conversation with someone you are calling back after receiving a message. First, you will listen to the voice message. Then the telephone call will begin. Each time it is your turn to speak, you will have 20 seconds to record. You should respond as fully and as appropriately as possible.

(Narrator)　　Listen to the voice message.

(Woman)　　もしもし、私、恵子。今日新宿で6時に待ち合わせしてたけど、急に行けなくなっちゃった。悪いけど、至急電話くれる？

(Narrator)　　Now the telephone call will begin. After the phone is answered, begin with a greeting and then explain why you are calling.

(Woman)　　[Telephone] [Rings twice and picks up] もしもし、恵子です。

(20 seconds)

(Woman)　　実はね、彼氏から電話があってねえ。今晩一緒に映画に行かないかってデートに誘われたのよ。

(20 seconds)

(Woman)　　ごめんね。ねえねえ、教えて。私、彼氏の前に行くと、緊張して何も言えなくなっちゃうのよ。どうしたらいいと思う？

(20 seconds)

(Woman)　　本当にごめんね。この埋め合わせ絶対にするから、今日は許して。この週末はどう？私がごちそうするから。

(20 seconds)

スクリプト：留守番電話

＜3・話す（留守番電話）＞

Return Telephone Call: Karaoke

15点
20秒 x 4

You will participate in a simulated telephone conversation with someone you are calling back after receiving a message. First, you will listen to the voice message. Then the telephone call will begin. Each time it is your turn to speak, you will have 20 seconds to record. You should respond as fully and as appropriately as possible.

(Narrator)   Listen to the voice message.

(Woman)   もしもし、由美だけど、今晩のカラオケの件で、相談したいことがあるから、至急、電話して。

(Narrator)   Now the telephone call will begin. After the phone is answered, begin with a greeting and then explain why you are calling.

(Woman)   [Telephone] [Rings twice and picks up] もしもし、由美ですが。

(20 seconds)

(Woman)   実はね、今晩のカラオケ、参加者がすごく増えちゃって、どうしようか。

(20 seconds)

(Woman)   そうね。それで、時間が6時からでしょ。夕食はどうしようか。

(20 seconds)

(Woman)   そうね。それがいいわね。ありがとう。じゃ、また。

(20 seconds)

<4・話す（留守番電話）>

Return Telephone Call: Community Service

15点
20秒 x 4

You will participate in a simulated telephone conversation with someone you are calling back after receiving a message. First, you will listen to the voice message. Then the telephone call will begin. Each time it is your turn to speak, you will have 20 seconds to record. You should respond as fully and as appropriately as possible.

(Narrator)   Listen to the voice message.

(Woman)   もしもし、中田ですが、週末のボランティア活動の件で、至急知らせたいことがあるから、電話して。

(Narrator)   Now the telephone call will begin. After the phone is answered, begin with a greeting and then explain why you are calling.

(Woman)   [Telephone] [Rings twice and picks up] もしもし、中田ですが。

(20 seconds)

(Woman)   この土曜日の午後、落書きを消すボランティアが必要なんだけど、行けそう？

(20 seconds)

(Woman)   そう、あと10人集めなくちゃいけないんだけど、どうしたら10人も集められるかなあ。いい考えない？

(20 seconds)

(Woman)   そうだね。じゃ、そうする。ありがとう。

(20 seconds)

スクリプト：留守番電話

＜５・話す（留守番電話）＞

Return Telephone Call: College Decisions

15点
20秒 x 4

You will participate in a simulated telephone conversation with someone you are calling back after receiving a message. First, you will listen to the voice message. Then the telephone call will begin. Each time it is your turn to speak, you will have 20 seconds to record. You should respond as fully and as appropriately as possible.

(Narrator)	Listen to the voice message.
(Man)	もしもし、上田ですが、すぐ知らせたいニュースがあるから、すぐ電話して。
(Narrator)	Now the telephone call will begin. After the phone is answered, begin with a greeting and then explain why you are calling.
(Man)	[Telephone] [Rings twice and picks up] もしもし、上田ですが。

(20 seconds)

(Man)　　　実はね、入りたかった桜大学に合格出来たんだよ。

(20 seconds)

(Man)　　　だけど、授業料が高くて、どうしようか心配しているんだ。

(20 seconds)

(Man)　　　そうだよね。そうしてみるよ。ありがとう。

(20 seconds)

スクリプト：留守番電話

＜6・話す（留守番電話）＞

15点
20秒 x 4

Return Telephone Call: Dance Party

You will participate in a simulated telephone conversation with someone you are calling back after receiving a message. First, you will listen to the voice message. Then the telephone call will begin. Each time it is your turn to speak, you will have 20 seconds to record. You should respond as fully and as appropriately as possible.

(Narrator)   Listen to the voice message.

(Girl)   もしもし、まり子だけど、ダンスパーティーのことで相談があるんだ。すぐ電話してくれない？

(Narrator)   Now the telephone call will begin. After the phone is answered, begin with a greeting and then explain why you are calling.

(Girl)   [Telephone] [Rings twice and picks up] もしもし、まり子ですが。

(20 seconds)

(Girl)   実は、ケンにダンスパーティーに誘(さそ)われたの。私、びっくりしちゃった。

(20 seconds)

(Girl)   それで、どんな格好(かっこう)をして行ったらいいと思う？

(20 seconds)

(Girl)   いいね。そうしてみる。じゃ、またね。

(20 seconds)

スクリプト：留守番電話   240

<7・話す（留守番電話）>

Return Telephone Call: Cellular Phone

15点
20秒 x 4

You will participate in a simulated telephone conversation with someone you are calling back after receiving a message. First, you will listen to the voice message. Then the telephone call will begin. Each time it is your turn to speak, you will have 20 seconds to record. You should respond as fully and as appropriately as possible.

(Narrator)   Listen to the voice message.

(Man)   もしもし、ケンだけど、これ、友達のケータイなんだ。この電話番号に至急、電話して。

(Narrator)   Now the telephone call will begin. After the phone is answered, begin with a greeting and then explain why you are calling.

(Man)   [Telephone] [Rings twice and picks up] もしもし、ケンですが。

(20 seconds)

(Man)   実は、授業中にケータイを使っていたら、先生に取り上げられちゃったんだよ。

(20 seconds)

(Man)   それに、先生、もう帰っちゃったし、どうしたらいいと思う？

(20 seconds)

(Man)   そうだね。そうしてみる。ありがとう。

(20 seconds)

スクリプト：留守番電話

＜８・話す（留守番電話）＞

Return Telephone Call: Speech

15点
20秒 x 4

You will participate in a simulated telephone conversation with someone you are calling back after receiving a message. First, you will listen to the voice message. Then the telephone call will begin. Each time it is your turn to speak, you will have 20 seconds to record. You should respond as fully and as appropriately as possible.

(Narrator)   Listen to the voice message.

(Woman)   もしもし、坂本ですが、今晩の日本クラブの会のスピーチのことで、ちょっと問題が生じましたから、お電話下さい。

(Narrator)   Now the telephone call will begin. After the phone is answered, begin with a greeting and then explain why you are calling.

(Woman)   [Telephone] [Rings twice and picks up] もしもし、坂本ですが。

(20 seconds)

(Woman)   実は、今晩スピーチをするはずだった生徒が、熱を出してお休みなんですよ。

(20 seconds)

(Woman)   それで、スピーチの原稿(げんこう)もないんですよ。どうしたらいいでしょうかねえ。

(20 seconds)

(Woman)   あ、そうですね。じゃ、そうしてみましょう。じゃ、今晩よろしくお願いします。

(20 seconds)

＜9・話す（留守番電話）＞

Return Telephone Call: Christmas Cake

15点
20秒 x 4

You will participate in a simulated telephone conversation with someone you are calling back after receiving a message. First, you will listen to the voice message. Then the telephone call will begin. Each time it is your turn to speak, you will have 20 seconds to record. You should respond as fully and as appropriately as possible.

(Narrator)   Listen to the voice message.

(Woman)   もしもし、植村です。今、車からなんだけど、クリスマスパーティーに間に合いそうにないから、電話して。

(Narrator)   Now the telephone call will begin. After the phone is answered, begin with a greeting and then explain why you are calling.

(Woman)   [Telephone] [Rings twice and picks up] もしもし、植村ですが。

(20 seconds)

(Woman)   あのね、実は、今運転している道路、工事をやっているみたいで、渋滞して、全然動けないんだけど。

(20 seconds)

(Woman)   それで、アイスクリームのクリスマスケーキがトランクの中にあって、溶けそうで、心配なんだ。どうしよう？

(20 seconds)

(Woman)   そうだね。そうしてみる。ありがとう。じゃね。

(20 seconds)

スクリプト：留守番電話

<10・話す（留守番電話）>

Return Telephone Call: Hiking

You will participate in a simulated telephone conversation with someone you are calling back after receiving a message. First, you will listen to the voice message. Then the telephone call will begin. Each time it is your turn to speak, you will have 20 seconds to record. You should respond as fully and as appropriately as possible.

(Narrator)　　Listen to the voice message.

(Man)　　もしもし、ケンだけど、明日のハイキングの計画を変更しなくちゃいけないから、至急、電話して。

(Narrator)　　Now the telephone call will begin. After the phone is answered, begin with a greeting and then explain why you are calling.

(Man)　　[Telephone] [Rings twice and picks up] もしもし、ケンです。

(20 seconds)

(Man)　　実は、天気予報によると、明日、大雨らしいんだよ。

(20 seconds)

(Man)　　それで、ハイキングのかわりに、何をしたらいいと思う？

(20 seconds)

(Man)　　あ、そうだね。それがいいね。じゃ、明日。

(20 seconds)

スクリプト：留守番電話

<11・話す（留守番電話）>

Return Telephone Call: Pizza

15点
20秒 x 4

You will participate in a simulated telephone conversation with someone you are calling back after receiving a message. First, you will listen to the voice message. Then the telephone call will begin. Each time it is your turn to speak, you will have 20 seconds to record. You should respond as fully and as appropriately as possible.

(Narrator)　　Listen to the voice message.

(Man)　　もしもし、レインボーピザですが、ご注文のピザの件で、至急ご連絡下さい。

(Narrator)　　Now the telephone call will begin. After the phone is answered, begin with a greeting and then explain why you are calling.

(Man)　　[Telephone] [Rings twice and picks up] もしもし、毎度ありがとうございます。レインボーピザです。

(20 seconds)

(Man)　　あのう、大変申し訳ないのですが、配達中にタイヤがパンクしてしまったんです。

(20 seconds)

(Man)　　それで、お時間までにお届け出来ないので、どうしたら、いいでしょうか。

(20 seconds)

(Man)　　ありがとうございます。では、そうさせていただきます。

(20 seconds)

スクリプト：留守番電話

<12・話す（留守番電話）>

15点
20秒 x 4

Return Telephone Call: Department Store

You will participate in a simulated telephone conversation with someone you are calling back after receiving a message. First, you will listen to the voice message. Then the telephone call will begin. Each time it is your turn to speak, you will have 20 seconds to record. You should respond as fully and as appropriately as possible.

(Narrator)　　　Listen to the voice message.

(Woman)　　　もしもし、花丸デパートでございます。カメラをお探しと伺いました。至急、ご連絡下さい。

(Narrator)　　　Now the telephone call will begin. After the phone is answered, begin with a greeting and then explain why you are calling.

(Woman)　　　[Telephone] [Rings twice and picks up] もしもし、花丸デパートでございます。

(20 seconds)

(Woman)　　　あのう、どんなカメラをお探(さが)しですか。

(20 seconds)

(Woman)　　　そうですか。実は、似(に)たようなカメラをお預(あず)かりしております。いかがいたしましょうか。

(20 seconds)

(Woman)　　　では、そうさせていただきます。ありがとうございます。

(20 seconds)

スクリプト：留守番電話

<13・話す（留守番電話）>

Return Telephone Call: Japan Trip

15点
20秒x4

You will participate in a simulated telephone conversation with someone you are calling back after receiving a message. First, you will listen to the voice message. Then the telephone call will begin. Each time it is your turn to speak, you will have 20 seconds to record. You should respond as fully and as appropriately as possible.

(Narrator) Listen to the voice message.

(Man) もしもし、カイだけど、すっごくいいニュースがあるから、すぐ電話して。

(Narrator) Now the telephone call will begin. After the phone is answered, begin with a greeting and then explain why you are calling.

(Man) [Telephone] [Rings twice and picks up] もしもし、カイです。

(20 seconds)

(Man) 実は、コンテストで勝って、日本に行けることになったんだ。

(20 seconds)

(Man) だけど、日本語でスピーチしなくちゃいけないんだ。おれ、人前で話すの苦手だから。

(20 seconds)

(Man) そうだよな。じゃ、そうするよ。ありがとう。

(20 seconds)

スクリプト：留守番電話

REFERENCES

AP Japanese Language and Culture Course Description, College Board, May 2007
マイロク先生の地球一よく分かる！温暖化問題　www.team-6.net/-6sensei/
中国新聞「ひろしま国」http://www.chugoku-np.co.jp/hiroshima-koku/
アロハウォーカー　http://www.alohawalker.com
フリープランエースJTB 南紀・伊勢志摩　http://www.jtb.co.jp/ace/cus/
味の素ゼネラルフーヅ株式会社「主婦の意識調査」